# DON'T SPILL THE TEA

*One Woman's Journey
From Abuse to Abundance*

**RHONDA A. THOMPSON**

*Foreword by*
**DR. MELVA HENDERSON**

DON'T SPILL THE TEA

Copyright © 2016 Rhonda A. Thompson

All rights reserved. No part of this book may be reproduced or transmitted in any form or by any means without written permission of the author.

ISBN: 978-0-9916015-9-2

Published By

# DEDICATION

This book is dedicated to those who have suffered abuse and loss. There are many who have been silenced forever. For you, I speak. I am "A Voice for the Voiceless".

For those that have survived to tell the story, be silent no more. I also dedicate this book to the countless children who are stuck in the cycle of abuse and those who have grown up believing that abusive behavior is normal.

A portion of the proceeds from this book will go to Rose of Sharon Transitional Living for Women Inc. to bring about awareness and an end to domestic violence. To learn more, visit

**WWW.ROSATL.ORG.**

You may not have survived domestic violence or sexual abuse but you have survived something, keep reading.

# FOREWORD

At the age of 16, I entered a relationship with a man named David. David was extremely handsome but he was also someone with unresolved issues. David was adopted at a very young age by an elderly couple that did their best to love and provide for him.

But David's internal struggles were deeper than anyone would ever know. I would quickly discover that at 17 years old David battled the demon called abandonment. All the symptoms were there. I was however young, and in love, so I ignored them all.

As our relationship grew, those symptoms turned into behaviors that became more and more controlling and unfortunately, abusive. What was once young love quickly shifted to a relationship filled with domination and fear. Eventually, I would become David's punching bag.

My face revealed black eyes, swollen lips, and a near concussion. I too know the horrors of domestic abuse and although freed from its grips, my life has been significantly impacted by it.

Domestic abuse is an age old problem that affects millions of women and surprisingly men annually within the United States alone. Domestic violence is the silent killer that few are willing to talk about.

Through the ashes of physical and sexual abuse, Rhonda Thompson has risen. No longer afraid to tell her story, Rhonda is becoming a leading voice of advocacy for domestic violence in our nation, particularly among women. Her beauty and grace draws women to her but her willingness to be open and transparent about something affecting so many keeps them coming back for more.

In this book, Don't Spill The Tea, Rhonda Thompson faces the fears and demons that have held women captive for many years. She shares her own story of abuse and neglect so that readers understand the root of her passion to inform and free others. Rhonda takes us on a journey that makes us laugh and cry and one that gives us the necessary tools for recovery.

For more than 20 years, I've walked with Rhonda Thompson. I know her and I know her story. It's one of neglect and abuse but also one of great victory. I've been there when the trauma of her past was trying to steal the promise of her future.

I've watched as she pushed to do the necessary work moving toward healing while creating a platform of deliverance for someone else. Rhonda is authentic and **Don't Spill The Tea** can help all of us see that there truly is life after abuse.

*Dr. Melva L. Henderson*
*Vice President,*
*World Outreach Bible Training Center Inc.*
*Founder/President,*
*Melva Henderson Ministries/SOAR Int.*
*Milwaukee, WI*

# INTRODUCTION

My family had secrets that weakened the very essence of who I became. I lost my voice quite some time ago due to unspeakable trauma and I never quite knew if I would find the strength to get it back.

I now know that in order to regain our voices and rediscover our strength, we must spill the tea. The simple, yet powerful act of doing so allows us to become free from the weight that past heartaches can cause. Sometimes we are addicted to pain because that is the only way that we are able to feel. The pain and hurt that we are burdened with often makes us numb or immune to any other emotion.

Discomfort, hurt, and many of life's obstacles at least allow us to feel and recognize that we are in fact alive. Today, I stand as a survivor who has managed to still feel love in my heart. God so loved the world that he gave his only begotten son.

Through the power of God's love, I have a renewed sense of compassion for myself and others.

It is my hope that I never become desensitized to love and to forgiveness. It was in the midst of pain that I found my voice. I was determined to find a way to speak for so many who haven't yet found the strength to speak. I know your heart. I wrote this book because I wanted to take you on a journey with me through my pain and into my prosperity. But as I write these words to you, I reclaim my power by spilling the tea.

Insurmountable disappointment, neglect and abuse and abandonment have been the fuel to my fire; the fire that burns every fiber of dysfunction that plagued my life. As I write to you, I will now shed the layers and tell some never told before secrets. I have resolved to spill the tea.

Not only was I plagued by the embarrassment from my turmoil but also the embarrassment of my own sins. Right here and right now, in this moment, the tea is finally getting spilled. I wrote this story for the little girl that was not protected and who had to endure alone.

God is my healer and I am made whole with and in him! As we journey together becoming voices for the voiceless, we help others to live in their truth. I am thankful for all that I went through because it was the road map that God used to get me to this point.

No more secrets. I spill the tea for you and for those who are seeking freedom from their own closets. This is for the girl with an attitude because she has a chip on her shoulder; and the young lady who is angry because she was victimized but hasn't learned how to accept what has happened to her or how to respond with love.

Healing is my bread. I hunger no more. Nothing that has happened to me can continue to keep me from my purpose. I cry aloud: "NO MORE!" Say it with me: "NO MORE?" No more violence against women and children. Not only have I decided to walk in my truth by spilling the tea but I have also determined that my life's purpose is to inspire as well.

In this book, I provide guides and tools to help you deal with grief, forgiveness, reclaiming your worth and other inspirational and biblical principals that helped me to make it through. You are not alone.

So grab your wine, coffee or tea and sip along this journey with me. Prepare to laugh, cry, and be inspired. Unapologetically, I give my story to you.

*Don't run from pain.*

*In these moments, endurance is developed and the burden of the pressure that you feel eventually releases a diamond. Embrace everything life has to offer.*

*When you conquer, you rise.*

*You will be stronger and better than ever. Your best days will be ahead of you not behind you.*

*Claim this year as the year of enlarged territory and endless possibilities.*

Rhonda A. Thompson

# CHAPTER ONE:

*Beauty to Ashes: The Monster in My Closet*

I was born as La Rhonda Wright in Milwaukee, Wisconsin to a biracial family. My mother, Regina, was an 18-year-old African American woman, and my father, Angel, was an older Puerto Rican man. After my birth, my parents went in different directions and my mother remained a single parent for the duration of my childhood.

Growing up during those times, my parents learned to date within their own race and the consideration of any other options would cause issues for the family. My grandparents believed that my mother had lost her mind by getting pregnant from a Spanish speaking man.

My grandmother always referred to my father as such and there was a negative connotation regarding his relationship with my mother. Furthermore, there was even more disdain for a child born outside of marriage. This child was me. Consequently, they offered assistance to my mother while she raised me.

From what I was told, I was born ready for the world and did many things before my peers. I took my first steps beginning at seven months old and my grandmother thought that I was advanced.

Being biracial was only the beginning of my struggles. Kids laughed and talked about each other all the time and we called it "ranking". I was no exception to the rule. I was 4'11 with an athletic build and profound features.

In school I would often get teased about having a larger than life nose and lips. Kids said, "Rhonda nose everything". They also said some very mean things about what I did with my lips. My hair was not straightened and it was nappy to the core.

The mix of scrutiny and the uncertainty of my family life often made me question myself. This was the beginning of my identity struggles. I didn't feel beautiful. As a matter of fact, there were many times that I felt completely ugly. Beauty goes beyond what is seen with our eyes.

When I was a little girl, my mother and I were at a friend's house in Racine, WI. She had just gotten dressed. At this time, I was standing approximately three and a half to four feet tall. My mom had on something pretty, and I remember rubbing her hip.

For no apparent reason she pushed my hand down. I was immediately stricken with confusion and hurt. Her friend saw the hurt in my eyes and said to my mom "don't do that! She thinks you're beautiful".

As a little girl, you determine what is beautiful by using your mother as a reference. I believe that this is where confidence begins to develop. This defining moment was the beginning of my search for beauty and acceptance. At the time, neither of us realized that my mom would soon go through one of the most devastating events in her life.

We would later learn that my mother was in the beginning phase of undiagnosed mental illness. She was only around 25 years old at this time. My search for beauty and acceptance continued. As young as I was, I truly had very little understanding of my mother's condition. This created walls within me and like many, I was in need of love.

I was very lonely without the love and comfort of my mother. As a little girl, you haven't yet developed what love means to you, yet, something inside allows you to feel and to recognize if you have it or not.

I began to realize just how much my grandparents filled in the gaps where my mother and father lacked, but the words "I love you" and the hugs and kisses were very scarce.

I was the same as many normal little girls. I ran and played and jumped and had friends. I always wanted to play with the toys that bigger kids played with. I traded my Barbie dolls for a Monopoly game. I also ran track and raced bikes with the boys.

I climbed fences and trees, and I hung on the porch and played hide and seek. I also planned all the candy parties in my grandparents' basement. In retrospect, the only major difference between me and other little girls my age, was that I liked doing the things that boys liked to do.

Back then, I was a tomboy, and today I am uber feminine. I never had dreams of being married or having the house with the white picket fence. Quite possibly, because I was lonely and pained, these were not things that I envisioned. Because my mother wasn't the example of a woman that I sought after, I began seeking my identity in other areas. The real truth is that I didn't have much to choose from.

When my step mother was introduced into my life, I remember recognizing that she was very beautiful.

I didn't however see very much of her prior to my deciding that I liked to hang with the boys.

I had this crazy obsession that Diana Ross would be my mother and rescue me from the world I lived in.

Since my hair resembled hers, I would take my hair down and comb it out and spin around the room with laughter at the notion that one day I would become the daughter of Diana Ross. I guess you could say that I was a silly little girl.

Don't get me wrong, when things were good, my mother would buy me elaborate gifts and toys. I can remember one Christmas that under the tree was filled with amazing gifts. And even though that is everything a child could hope for, I can't recall my mother sitting to play with me. I guess the toys were her way of showing love.

## *The Mind*

It is without question that my mother was beautiful; however I seemed to have missed so many opportunities to discover beauty with her. It wasn't until recently that I understood that she was clearly incapable of giving me what she didn't have. My mother was an educated woman who served our country with pride.

However, her lack of love and understanding of what a child needed left me completely broken and bruised emotionally. There are so many times I can remember her tangents and outbursts. As a latchkey kid, my mom arrived home from work late. If she were in a bad mood, I would get hit.

A spanking is what some call it; however, as a mother myself, I understand that what she rendered was far more than that.

My mom heard voices and would talk to herself for hours on end. I would be completely terrified of what I was witnessing. I was so young. There were many days that I wouldn't eat a balanced meal or even worse, the food that she did cook was still bleeding on my plate.

Even in the midst of my turmoil, I thank God for his covering. The trauma that I endured is still very fresh in my mind and even in sharing this story with you, I am healing. There was a time when I got into trouble for something I did, and my mom threw a can of starch across the room at me. It was in moments like this that I learned how to run track. Ha! She was always angry with me. In her anger I learned to find comfort within. I was so afraid of her. The voices in her head were violent and told her that I was a dog and I recognize this as weird but it is my truth.

Imagine being yelled at for barking too loud and constantly told to stop barking. I couldn't have possibly answered for what was going on in her mind. I was her only daughter, and she recognized me as a dog? Why would I bark when all I wanted was to be loved as a daughter? Beyond all of the feelings of insecurity, I just didn't understand, nor did I feel safe.

I wasn't the only one who was concerned about my well being. My aunt and grandfather taught me how to get help if I needed to.

They also taught me how to run, and I ran away often. Things even got so bad that my aunt gave me $3.00 and told me to keep it in case of an emergency, or if I needed to call or take the bus. Back then, that amount was sufficient to save my life.

Around age six or seven years old, the spankings turned to beatings. I would cry out so loud "Mamma, please stop! I won't do it again". I never even knew what it was that I had done. On one occasion, she had beaten me before attending school. I attended a private Lutheran school where I also received physical punishments. Back then, schools did not notify the police or child protection services unless the child requested.

On this particular day, we had school photos, and I had a large raw, round scar on my face. After the photos, they added a bandage to my face to cover the scar. When I arrived at home, my mom ripped the bandage off my face. My heart sank into my feet, and my soul was torn from my chest. I screamed and cried so profusely that the tears from my eyes burned the scar. I still remember the sting in my heart and on my face.

I learned that day that no one would hear me and no one would help me. I was overcome with loneliness. Nonetheless, I stopped crying when I went to my room and started day dreaming of another place where I could go and be loved.

## *Psalms 27:10*

*When my father and my mother forsake me, then the LORD will take me up.*

I didn't know God then but one day I would. My mother was the only source of life I had; she had the ability to clothe, feed, house, and reward me at any time. I did everything I could to comply with her wishes and desires.

Because she was the first monster in my closet I lived in terror. When I would go to bed at night, I had nightmares of falling into an endless pit. I somehow thought it would be better if I made it to the bottom.

## *Capture the Monster*

Eventually, my family figured out that there was something wrong with my mother. I thought that she would finally get help! Her trip to the hospital did not go down without a fight. My uncles had to subdue her many times. She was so strong that it took two to three men to hold her down, and at times, they had to punch and restrain her.

This was another instance in which I experienced even more abuse. Even though I understood what they were doing and why; this still was my mom and to see her in an arrested state was even scarier.

She was a trapped animal, unable to be free. As ironic as it sounds, I was sad and happy at the same time. I was sad that my mom was captured, but I was happy that the monster wouldn't hurt me again.

I often wondered how her absence would affect me. I ended up in a foster home for a very short time until my family came up with a plan. My uncles decided that the best place for me was with them. Three of my four uncles shared the responsibility of raising me along with my grandparents. I was on a rotation system for awhile. Some homes were better than others. Some cousins were much more fun to hang with than others.

My mother was diagnosed with Maniac Depression but finding the correct medication meant a lifelong search for her and constant abuse for me. As I grew to know and understand my mother's condition, I became angry.

I learned around 8 years old or so how to protect myself and what I needed to do if her alter ego showed up. This sequence went on for years.

One day as I was getting out of school, my mother showed up unannounced to pick me up. I was so embarrassed because she had that look in her eyes. I didn't let her know that I saw her. I ran as fast as I could and got on the bus and hid for dear life. How awful!

This time in elementary school was mortifying for me. We moved so much that I ended up in a total of 8 different elementary schools by 5th grade. My father remained in my life during this time with hopes of gaining full custody of me. I visited him twice each month. My grandmother wasn't a big fan of my dad, and I know that it had something to do with the fact that he was older than my mother and that he was of a different race.

I didn't care; I just wanted a mommy and daddy. And although, I try to remember good times with my dad, it was all a lie because he wasn't aware of the abuse from my mother.

### *Inspirational IV*

*What is forgiveness?*

Forgiveness is the act of pardoning an offender. It doesn't mean that one will forget but it does mean you don't hold the offender prisoner to the sin. You must release and let go. In the end you will be free.

To harbor unforgiveness means you give power and energy to the offender thus exhausting and hindering your own progress. The offender has moved on and you are stuck in time and pain, living a life without the true abundance God intended for you to have.

Forgiveness doesn't mean reconciliation to the offender or condoning the actions. This is where many fail to forgive and get stuck.

## *Hebrews 12:1*

*Therefore, since we are surrounded by such a huge crowd of witnesses to the life of faith, let us strip off every weight that slows us down, especially the sin that so easily trips us up. And let us run with endurance the race God has set before us.*

## *Ten Myths About Forgiveness*

1. You have to forget.
2. You must accept the behavior of the offender.
3. Forgiveness is a feeling not an action.
4. You must get over being hurt.
5. You can't forgive a repeated offense.
6. Forgiveness means that you are saying that what happened is ok.
7. Forgiveness means that the person was not sorry.
8. Forgiveness makes you look weak.
9. Forgiveness means that they are free to hurt you again.
10. You must only forgive those that you want to stay in relationship with.

*"Choose to forgive.
The burden is too expensive
for you to pay."*

Rhonda A. Thompson

## *Forgiveness is a Choice*

Forgiveness is a process. To begin this process, we must ask ourselves the following questions:

**How do I forgive?**

**Who do I need to forgive?**

**Step One:**

*Make a decision to be better.*

I, _____, deserve a happy full life.

**Step Two:**

*Share your experiences with a trusted advisor and practice articulating the offense. Come to terms that it wasn't your fault. I can trust _____ to share my feelings with.*

**Step Three:**

*Release the expectation of being in control. Select a circle of people that will love and not hurt or re-victimize you.*

**Step Four:**

*Practice being free from the bondage of the victimization. This is when self-love and positive actions towards others are exemplified.*

**Step Five:**

Today (date)_____I choose to forgive. I am free!

# CHAPTER TWO:

*Spilling the Tea*

In the Southern regions of the US, we often use the term "spill the tea". It means to share an especially juicy bit of gossip. No one has the ability to gossip about this little girl anymore because I have reclaimed my voice and spilled my own tea. When my mother would get angry at me, she would firmly call me by my legal name, La Rhonda.

This left me utterly scared for life. Even today, I don't allow anyone to call me by that name. It reminds me of one of the most tumultuous times in my life. The abuse at my mother's hands would go into the teen years of my life.

My dad remained in my life during this time. Handsome and statuesque in nature, he stood at about 5'8. His Puerto Rican heritage was worn proudly like a badge of honor and could be seen in his glorious afro that made many envious.

In the 70s, the bigger the afro, the bigger the ego. He was a salsa musician in a band. He played many instruments, including the maracas, congas, bongos and timbales. Because of his skills, he was named "Paleco" in honor of the famous Latin percussionist.

My dad would do his fatherly duties by picking me up on the weekends and allowing me to experience a different way of life. He would take me to his sister's house to visit often. Back then, interracial families were not celebrated. My visits at my aunt's house didn't produce the best memories.

I can remember the other kids not wanting to play with me while there. My dad really wanted me to integrate with his family, and I tried hard to be a part. I didn't speak Spanish, so I stood out like a sore thumb. I hated going to visit because I was already dealing with my mom and her dysfunctional disposition. This was added insult to injury. My dad didn't have any other children at that time so I would be really bored while visiting.

My father found love with a lady by the name of Karen and got married. At his home, I did, however, look forward to spending time with his wife. She exemplified femininity and beauty to me.

She would do my hair and talk to me like I imagined a mother would. I enjoyed my time with her. She was refreshing to me. She smelled of sweet perfume and dressed really nice. Karen would look forward to my company as well. She was only 17 years old when she got married to my dad. He was the first man she had known. She was good to both my father and me.

I was also surprised at how well Karen cooked. She would always buy Yoplait Yogurt, and I couldn't wait to get to my dad's home to enjoy it. Black cherry was my favorite flavor. Sometimes the little things bring us joy and in the midst of my hardships, this was one of them. Karen's mom and family adored me, and they spoiled me rotten. I felt a sense of pride to be accepted as a part of her family.

I really felt as though life with my dad and Karen was a reprieve from the abuse that I experienced at home with my mother. That was wishful thinking. Even in all his glory I would later learn that he too had some deep-rooted issues that would affect me adversely. The abuse shifted gears a little. I can remember a time that Karen made dinner.

As I sat down at the table, I noticed she made a grilled cheese sandwich and tomato soup; this was my favorite meal. I was so excited and I know that this was apparent as I sat down at the table. Just as I got settled in my chair, my dad took my plate and switched it with his plate of liver and onions. My dad knew that I didn't like liver and onions, but for some strange reason he forced me to eat it.

He took my grilled cheese sandwich and ate it in front of me while I sat at the table. I cried for what felt like an eternity. I choked trying to eat his meal.

I felt so alone and neglected. I didn't see this as my dad teaching me a lesson; I received this as an inhumane act and another moment in which I wasn't loved. Even today, this memory still makes me gag. I never ate liver after that day and as an adult became a vegetarian. This was the first time I witnessed the monster in my daddy's house.

You may be reading this and thinking to yourself that there is nothing wrong with a father teaching his daughter to eat a variety of meals or to simply be thankful that there is food on the table. This was a trigger for me that I was all too familiar with. In these moments, I did not feel safe nor loved. Even at a young age, I recognized that if you love someone you don't force them to do things that they don't want to do.

Children can easily identify love, compassion and concern for their well being. Children also have the God given sense to know when they are in danger.

Often adults speak to children about the boogieman as an imaginary character or figment of their imagination. For me, the boogieman was in the next room. My dad had a problem with alcohol and he was also running from some demons of his past. One evening my dad was drinking while he was putting me to bed.

This evening wasn't like any of the other evenings. Something about the air was different. As he was taking my clothes off, I felt butterflies in my tummy. My dad's hands did something that I couldn't explain or comprehend.

I found myself really close to him, and he began kissing me on my neck and my chest. He then began sucking all over my little flat chest. Karen was just in the next bedroom, and we were separated by one wall. I didn't understand what was happening. I didn't know how to feel. I felt his sharp mustache on my fragile skin. I can still smell his breath, even today. I can't get this out of my head or senses.

I must admit that as I write this, fear makes me want to stop, but I call on God for the comfort that only he can give me. This was the only time that I can remember seeing this boogie monster, but the memories I won't soon forget. As an adult woman, I struggle sexually. I am not aroused by things that make most women excited. Even my breasts have to be caressed in a very careful way, or I can't move forward with my husband.

That night changed me forever. After that night, all of my fears of being alone in the world were confirmed. La Rhonda was alone and without a mommy or daddy. There was no protection for me in this world.

After that night, I would encounter and suffer sexual abuse from other family members. One day while in my grandmothers' care I was taking a bath and she came in the bathroom and said "Oh my goodness, what's wrong with your chest?" I said "I don't know." Sadly, I knew that she was referring to the fact that one of my breasts had begun to develop while the other had not.

As the years passed after the abuse, I would visit him but I always remained very close to his wife. I didn't allow myself to be alone with him for fear that it would happen again. In retrospect, I realized that the pain that my father caused me when I was a child was due to his sickness. He was an alcoholic and I was a casualty of his internal war.

I resolved to pick up the pieces of my life and move forward. I separated myself from my dad and the monster that I had tried so hard to escape.

I eventually reached one of the biggest milestones in my life: graduating. I worked hard within myself to find a source of forgiveness. In doing so, God encouraged my heart to invite him to experience this moment in time with me. I was happy to invite my father and I later learned that he was absolutely thrilled at the prospect of reuniting. His other children didn't understand why he desperately wanted to attend, but they all did.

On October 14, 2014 after leaving my graduation in Atlanta, GA, my dad made it back to Milwaukee, WI. He phoned to let me know that he had arrived back home safely. About five minutes after speaking with him, my phone rang. It was my brother informing me that my father had been hit by a car while walking the dog. He did not survive.

For 29 years we did not have a relationship and with a snap of fate, it had all ended. It hurt me deeply that all I had was one day to express my forgiveness. When his family picked up his phone, my last text message was still on the screen. It read "I love you, you look so good."

Years prior to my graduation, I told him that I forgave him, but I still had no relationship with him. I pray that the invitation to the graduation was where he really received peace in knowing that all was forgiven. And while it is my belief that he found peace, I must admit that I was completely torn apart because I felt that the way everything unfolded was so unfair.

He is now free from this secret, and I am still learning to forgive. I don't believe that all abusers want to abuse. I don't believe that it was my dad's desire. My dad was an amazing man to his family and he did a lot of good for his community in spite of the monsters in his closet and now in mine.

As I share my story, I recognize that many still struggle with forgiveness. Forgiving someone is not for them, it is for you. We miss so many years of our lives when we are unable to forgive. I was estranged from my father for over two decades. The moment that I embraced true forgiveness, he was gone. For so long, I didn't recognize that forgiveness was not for anyone other than me. I encourage you to refrain from allowing the myths of forgiveness to hold you back from being free and from a possible relationship with someone who really should be in your life.

Often times, victims are afraid to disclose the abuse out of fear or rejection, hurting someone that is close to the abuser, or not being believed. Four years after my dad's death, I knew that I would eventually need to share this story in order to truly be free. However, there was still one person that I was concerned about hurting with this revelation, and that was Karen. I was concerned for his older children but also Karen because she suffered serious emotional hurt from his passing, and I could never get up enough nerve to tell her.

After writing this book, I resolved to tell her prior to its release. I booked a trip to Milwaukee for quality time and a candid conversation with Karen. And although this was the last piece to finding my voice, it was also the hardest. I questioned if she would abandon me or if she would call me a liar.

I wondered if she would suffer more emotional pain. I took all of this concern to be my responsibility. We went to one of her favorite restaurants. Karen always loved the finer things in life, and I was always a receiver of her selections.

On this day, I only opted for soup and salad because I had no clue how this was going to go. I had also asked my best friend, Cleo, to wait outside to scrape me off the floor, if needed. Before I even began to tell my story, Karen began to express how much she was saddened by the past issues that my father and I had been plagued by. This was a great ice breaker and to my suprise, the moment that I expressed what had happened, she immediately said "I believe you."

I continued to talk with her, and we both sat together trying to figure out my true age at the time of the abuse. She recollected that she was between the ages of 17 and 23. She was very apologetic for not protecting me and I let her know that she was never to blame. By the time of our conversation, I had truly forgiven and blamed no one.

My father died in peace knowing that all is well, and I wanted for Karen to be free from any condemnation. She told me that I had all of her support, and she encouraged me to use my voice as much as I could to help others. This was such a heavy load that was lifted from my spirit. All I could do was cry.

I felt so complete after disclosing what happened to me with Karen. The woman that I had looked up to all of my life, and who played the role of a mother in my life even after my father's death, validated me. I would have told this story anyway but there is no greater gift than to have the support of those who love you.

Karen stated that she was not aware of the abuse but that after my disclosure, it all made sense to her regarding my estranged relationship with my father. Karen was upset at my dad's actions, but she was also relieved to know that I had forgiven him and that we were both peaceful in the end.

## *Signs of Sexual Abuse & Assault*

Parents, be sure to empower your children by giving them a voice and teaching them to recognize the signs of abuse. Children are often reluctant to ask for help for fear of not being believed or because threats made by the abuser towards them or their loved ones. It is never too early to have these discussions.

Take time to teach your child the proper names for their body parts. Teach them to be proud of their bodies.

If they feel ashamed, they will not want to tell you that someone violated them. Many times parents don't want to be embarrassed by their child's shyness and force them to hug friends and family.

I believe that we must allow our children to feel safe on their own terms regarding being touched by others. Children that are free to speak openly with their parents will be more willing to share uncomfortable feelings.

## *Recognizing Abuse*

I conducted research on the signs and symptoms of abuse that parents should look for, and I discovered that if abuse is present some signs to look for are: change in your child's fun loving personality, appears to be withdrawn from normal activity, sudden bed wetting, fear of being alone, change in appetite, uncontrollable crying, sleeping problems, stranger anxiety, depression, victimization of others, not wanting to be at a certain person's home or ride in their car, physical signs of blood in the private area, trouble sitting down, difficulty walking or urinating, or discharge in the mouth, genitals or anus.

Other signs to watch for include: the child wanting to play sexual games or engagement in childhood masturbation.

As the child becomes ages 9 years and above, observance of signs of promiscuous activity, substance abuse, suicidal thoughts, anger or running away from home should also be considered. After reading the site, I realized that I exemplified around 90 percent of the symptoms on this list.

To learn more, visit:
WWW.CHILDMOLESTATIONVICTIMS.COM.

According to Crimes Against Children Research Center, 1 in 5 girls and 1 in 20 boys are sexually abused by the age 18.

*When you are bound by abuse, spilling the tea isn't easy but necessary for your own freedom.*

Rhonda A. Thompson

## *Frame Your World With Your Words*

**REPEAT:**

*I will be silent no more. The hurt that another caused is NOT my fault.*

## *Generational Curses*

I often wondered why the abuse from both my mom and dad were attached to me. What was so imperfect about my lineage? God taught me that a tremendous part of my pain was what is often referred to as a generational curse. Unfortunately, much of what has happened to me is nothing different from many other little girls.

This period in time was a reflection of the pain in the hearts of my parents. With every new generation, the presence of past hurt and abuse have the potential to exist. One of my cousins later explained to me that my grandfather on my father's side of the family suffered a series of attacks. Some were the same demons that later plagued my life.

I couldn't believe that my grandfather whom I never met, was accused of molesting the children in the family, and this sickness almost killed him.

He was suicidal. This same curse was attempting to haunt me. I still don't have all the details but what I learned helped me to have compassion for my father. It was in the midst of compassion that Christ performed miracles.

Have you ever heard anyone say: "hurt people, hurt people?" I now understand this statement to be true.

Furthermore, I realize that my mother's mental illness was not her fault and that the secrets in her bloodline run deep as well. I never quite found out all that happened in the South where she was raised. And although I may never know the truth about my mother's hurt, I do know that she did not mean to hurt me the way she did.

Her remorse for the pain she caused me never touched my heart until much later in life. Today, I sympathize with the pain in my mother's eyes. I was her only child yet her own demons would not allow her to be successful in my rearing. Mental illness is something that goes undiagnosed for so many.

The results are often present in the abusing or even killing of others. In addition to that, denial and embarrassment often prevent us from reaching a diagnosis and path towards being healthy.

I was always embarrassed by my mother. Either she was talking to herself while walking down the street or showing up at my school and not looking her best.

She was often loud and violent while throwing away all of the contents in our house and leaving us with nothing. I just didn't understand and often wondered what would happen to me.

During this time my identity was completely suppressed. I was a child in danger.

I was angry, full of despair, hurt, and lonely. The constant state of confusion left me wondering how life would unfold for me. It all makes sense to me now. This was the beginning of the rest of my life and although there was so much darkness, the word of God gives us so much insight.

Jesus said, "Let the children come to me. Don't stop them! For the Kingdom of Heaven belongs to those who are like these children." This verse in Matthew 19:14 helped me to recognize that God had purpose for me.

## *Frame Your World With Your Words*

### REPEAT:

*No matter my beginning,*

*my end is destined for greatness.*

# CHAPTER THREE:

*Broken Vessel*

By the time I became a teenager, my life did not seem worth living. I ran away from home several times. My mother and I just couldn't get along. She was still trying to figure out her medication and was hospitalized most of my life. I was very angry. I dated every guy that I could. I was searching for love but only discovered more heartache and abuse.

One day when my mother and I were staying with my grandparents, my mom asked me to do something. I wasn't in the mood to do what she asked. I would often respond to her requests by informing her that she didn't raise me . On this day, my mother was not feeling my attitude. While I was sitting on the couch, she literally slapped the taste out of my mouth. The cookies that I had been preparing to eat went flying all over the living room. I slipped into an out of body experience.

On that day, I learned my strength. I cannot explain what came over me but I was numb. And as she was gathering the cookies, I stood up, tapped my mother on the shoulder, balled my right fist into a knot and punched her in the mouth.

She flew onto the sofa from the impact. While she was down, I reached for an antique glass lamp that sat next to the sofa in my grandmother's home.

As I reared back to hit my mother with it, my uncle had managed to grab my hand. I was released from the spell that I was under. I began to weep when I realized that I almost did some serious damage to my mother. She never hit me again after that day. The problem with this is that the tables turned and she now had fear of me. I knew she feared me and I lost even more control in my life. I was at the point of no return.

There wasn't anything that anyone could do to get my attention. By the time I turned 13 years old, I became sexually active. Truthfully, after I moved past the anxiety of the initial experience, it brought me a sense of relief. The problem was that I wasn't married, and I often felt even worse afterward. This didn't stop me.

In fact, I was active with multiple partners. My first real boyfriend was a gentle soul named Charles. Charles knew of the pain that I was dealing with. He was older than I. For my 13th birthday, he declared that it was time to introduce me to sex. He was under the impression that if I felt the closeness of someone else, maybe I wouldn't hurt so badly.

To me this seemed like a good idea, and it did bring me closer to him. This lesson was only to be a birthday present and nothing more, but I fell in love with him. Afterward, I recognized that he regretted his gift to me, and I just wanted more of him. Can you guess what he did? Yes girl, he ran for the hills.

After giving myself to Charles, who, mind you I thought was my boyfriend, he left me even more broken than before his attempt to help heal me. I never saw him again. Twenty-seven years later, Charles reached out to me on Facebook to say hello. I was polite and told him about all the amazing things happening in my life now.

I could read the tone in his message and I believe that he wished he hadn't done that to me and that he felt really bad. I forgave him a long time ago but it was good to see that he knew the damage that he had caused and that he took ownership.

Waiting for another boyfriend wasn't my cup of tea. I was in so much pain that a replacement was needed fairly quickly. I was very attractive and had a shape that many would die for. I had a flat tummy, glowing tight skin, breast that stood at attention and a butt that wouldn't quit. Without delay the next man in my life would prove to be a bad boy.

But the way that he would hold me in his arms made me feel rescued. When I was with him, the images of my past seemed to fade. His name was Fred. Fred was a bonafide gangster. All we did was have sex, fight and shop. Fred was verbally abusive to me and he would always tell me that no one would want me because my nose was too big. Fred eventually ending up going to jail and yes, I visited that fool.

Back then, where I came from, it was cool to stand by your man. Even though he was a cheater and he was abusive and gave me a sexually transmitted disease, I thought he loved me. While he was in jail, he proclaimed his undying love for me and told me that if I stayed with him, he would marry me. He also told me that he would not hurt me ever again. My loyalty to him lasted about five months or so until I realized that there were other fish in the sea.

Within that same year I met James. He was so handsome that all the girls liked him. He was a bit older than

I and again I found myself on a high from dating an older man. James broke my heart so badly that the scar from our relationship lasted well into my 30s. There was no pain like the pain I felt from being with James. During our six month, long term relationship, I thought that I had arrived. I had never been with anyone this long.

James and I did everything together. We even wore matching outfits. And because James sold drugs I got the latest shoes and clothing. James and I took professional pictures, and I was his girl. At least, I thought that I was.

I also thought that because of our relationship, there would be no other women involved. The violent demeanor that I then possessed left no room for James' interest in any other girls. This went on for a while. Back then we used beepers or what some referred to as "pagers" to communicate.

If I paged him and he didn't call me back within a certain amount of time, I would ensure that he recognized my disdain. James started to retaliate against me. The yelling and pushing quickly changed to slapping and strangling. I thought that James really loved me.

After he was violent, he would tell me that he loved me and that I just needed to calm down. He assured me that I had nothing to worry about and that his loyalty was with me. I would cry and he would hold me close while kissing my face and telling me all the things that a girl would want to hear. After overcoming the storm that raged within our relationship and witnessing the rainbow, the cycle of abuse would rain down again.

During the good times, James would give me gifts and we would have make up sex. One day I found out that I was pregnant. I was only 13 years old. Yes, pregnant with my first child at 13. I was actually excited that James and I were going to be family. I had no clue how to be a mother or create a family unit, but I did know that I would qualify for government assistance.

With this information, I made plans for James and I to get an apartment and finally be together full time. All I could think about was that I would no longer have to wonder if he were cheating on me because I would be in the same house with him and I would know. Although, I really enjoyed dating an older man, I did not know that there would be a price to pay when rushing the process.

During my pregnancy, I started to feel ill. I slept all day and couldn't go to school. One day I was overtaken with cramps. I was in so much pain that all I could do was scream. I went into the bathroom and the unthinkable happened; I lost the baby.

Although I had never been pregnant, my spirit knew what happened. The agony plagued my soul. I screamed "James, James, please help me our baby is gone!" Even as a child experiencing the loss of one is a pain that I can never articulate.

I wasn't ready to be a mother, but I welcomed the opportunity to birth someone into this world that would have loved me back, unconditionally.

For so many years, I lived with such a broken heart. But the heavenly father saw fit to bring his angel home. The bond between James and I grew even stronger. We had now shared loss together. For some reason, I still felt insecure and didn't trust him because he had cheated on me before.

The day after being released from the hospital, I called him, and he didn't answer. He told me that he would be at home so I tried him several more times. Finally, I called a cab to take me to his house. I could barely walk from the lingering cramps after the loss of our baby. I was bleeding profusely when I arrived at his house.

From the window, I could see people moving around in his bedroom upstairs. I didn't hesitate to confront the activity. To my surprise, the front door was open. I stormed upstairs screaming and crying "Who is this?"

"I just lost our baby and this is what you do to me?" He pushed me several times telling me to get the hell out of his house while another young lady who was there with him watched. I was not afraid of

him and I was full of rage from my emotions.

Him pushing me couldn't compare to the level of betrayal that I was experiencing at that time.

I questioned myself in that moment wondering why my life was such a disaster. At 13 years old, I had witnessed and been a part of more dysfunction than some are exposed to in a lifetime, but I still made an effort to do some activities that were age appropriate.

Outside of my dysfunctional life, I was an athlete. I ran track, raced bikes and danced. I loved to dance, but I hated school. Any excuse to skip was cool with me. I had reserved my pregnancy as a ticket to stay at home. Now that it was over, the desire to do the things I loved so much started to slowly fade away.

Depression became my new comfort. I embraced it because it allowed me to feel. I wasn't very comfortable talking to others about my feelings, and I bottled the layers of pain inside. I managed life by having sex. I was often numb to the act, but at least I was being loved. This was wrong on so many levels. Even when I had not protected myself, God never ceased to wrap his loving arms of protection around me.

# CHAPTER FOUR:
*The Medication, The Mask*

After losing the baby and finding James cheating on me again, I just couldn't take it. I had already begun drinking, but now, I was drinking more regularly. One day, my life flashed before me, and I reached my breaking point. I had dealt with abuse from my mother and father, from the man I loved and I just couldn't understand how life was supposed to be good for me. It made no sense. I was in a complete state of depression.

I introduced myself to the medicine cabinet and all of my mother's meds. That day, I took 23 sleeping pills. I did not leave a note. This was deliberate and not for attention. James made a surprise visit to my house and thank God that he did. He had threatened my life on so many occasions in one way or another but that day, he saved my life.

My mother let him in and when he came to my room, I was passed out. He started shaking me and yelling my name. "Rhonda, Rhonda, what's wrong with you girl?" I even remember feeling a slap to my face a few times.

He was trying to get me to a coherent state because it was clear that something was critically wrong. I tried opening my eyes, and I remember hearing him ask: "what did you do?" I motioned towards the floor and removed the blanket that revealed an empty bottle of sleeping pills.

My speech was slurred, and I was quite delusional. I remember this as if it were yesterday.

Laying there in his arms, I started speaking of a time when I was most happy with him. In the midst of my slumber, I recounted a photo shoot that he and I had done together. I was making odd statements like "8x10." James didn't understand.

He hurried and advised my mother to call 911, and I was rushed to the hospital. While I recall the hospital staff pouring charcoal down my throat and pumping my stomach, I got sick and vomited the charcoal back up. It was all over me, on the floor, and on the bed. I imagine that it looked like something from the Exorcist.

Getting your stomach pumped is no fun; it was painful and because I was so sedated I was also dizzy. The pain from the doctors pushing that tube down my throat was very scary. I choked during the entire process. I was hallucinating and saying things that made no sense. James was right by my bed side.

I remember thinking that he must love me. I asked James to take me home, and I told him that I was sorry. I also told him that I would not do this to myself again. James agreed to take me home and left the room to find out what the procedure for discharge would be. When he came back, he advised me that I would not be going home and that the hospital had made the decision to keep me. As I was being rolled away, I cried and screamed for James.

What I didn't know was that when you try to take your life, you are not released without a psychiatric evaluation. I had no clue that I would be spending the next week in a mental institution for teens. And while the rest of the world thought that I was crazy; I was really in need of a break from life.

During my time in the mental ward, I was forced to participate in peer groups. I just couldn't deal with it. There were kids there that were really mentally sick. I thought I would forget about this episode but you can never forget the sound of the loud screeching voices that filled the ward. There were kids that called for their mothers all day and night. Kids were often given shots for not controlling themselves.

I knew better than to tell those people that I was just trying to get attention. It was really sad to see the type of demons that young people were dealing with. These kids were frustrated. Some heard voices, and others couldn't control their bodily functions. I can't imagine not being able to control your thoughts or the voices inside your head. It is the word of God that keeps us balanced and our minds stable.

This was the breaking point for James and me. The relationship with James dissolved after that. I was over him and honestly, looking for my next addiction. By this time, I realized that something was crucially wrong with me, but I wasn't mature enough to get help nor did I have any elders that I felt comfortable confiding in.

I continued to travel along the same journey. In order to maintain my sanity and not return to the mental hospital, I learned how to master the art of living behind a mask. I was so broken. To tell someone what I was dealing with would mean exposing my truths. The abusive relationships did not stop.

When I turned 14 years old, I was dating an older man named, Big Chuck. He was very abusive and our relationship was very short.

I was told that Big Chuck was a pimp and if I didn't stop dating him, he would pimp me out as well. I'll admit that I didn't really believe it. He was handsome and smart, I was just too naive to recognize the signs.

One day I got sick of being abused. Big Chuck and I had returned to my house after a night out drinking and while sitting on the sofa, we got into a disagreement. He got upset and slapped me in my face. After being slapped, I slapped him back.

I thought that this would be the perfect moment to protect myself.

This train of thought had worked in my abusive relationship with my mom so I had no reason to believe that it would not work in this relationship with Big Chuck. Big Chuck thought that it was disrespectful for me to hit him back. He hit me so hard that he almost knocked my teeth out of my mouth. I was bleeding from my mouth.

I understood real fast that I had written a check that I could not cash. However, I also recognized that this may have been the last time that I ever got a chance to show him that I wasn't a punk. I jumped up with fear in my heart, tears in my eyes, and blood running down my face, and I just ran. He chased me through the kitchen and pushed my bedroom door open.

All of this was happening while my mother was in the next room. He grabbed me by my hair and dragged me to my bedroom. He threw me on the bed and with his hands around my neck, began squeezing tightly.

He warned me: "Rhonda, if you ever hit me back again, I will kill you. Do you understand?"

Nodding my head up and down I expressed that I understood. It was at that moment that I knew that I was in a really dangerous relationship and I needed to end it immediately! I had never heard of domestic violence before, but I did recognize a pattern of other men hitting me.

I started to believe that this was how a man expressed love and concern for you. I thought that if a man didn't hit you, it meant that he didn't care. However, I began to recognize the error in my thought process. This was the first time that anyone threatened to kill me.

Big Chuck opened my eyes and for the first time I was warned that, what was a simple slap, punch, or choking episode would eventually end my life if I didn't change my mind and process regarding the type of men I chose to date.

Big Chuck was the last straw for me. I didn't wait for him to change, I did.

And with that change, I would not be hit by another man again. As if James, Big Chuck and Fred were not enough, the series of abusive relationships affected my self-esteem adversely.

The cycles continued, and I was so low that I continued picking the same men in different bodies.

Sean and I dated for a short while. I spent much of my time getting drunk. It was the norm for me. And although Sean wasn't as old as the others, he too thought it was cool to hit me. I thought that I had improved my selection of men but I hadn't. My behavior got worse with alcohol as a leading factor.

I was really reckless with my sexual activity and got pregnant again. Sean, humiliated me and told all our friends of our sexual exploits and that the baby wasn't his. I was distraught yet again. I felt like a whore. As a matter of fact that's what Sean's friends and even Sean started calling me. I went into a deep depression again and had no plans to tell my family that just a year later after the first tragedy, that I was pregnant again. How careless could I be?

Sean had been sleeping around and I could have easily contracted HIV or HPV or some other disease because he did not care who he slept with. However, I was pregnant and didn't know what to do.

I decided that I wasn't woman enough to face the embarrassment of having a child with a man who disowned me as so many others had in times past. I was sick to take ownership of my decision to terminate the pregnancy, but it was the right choice for me at the time. I got money from my family and I went alone.

As a child myself I had to endure all the ridicule from protestors. I remember walking past people swearing, holding up signs and telling me that I can make it and to trust them not to make such a critical decision. I pushed past the crowd with tears in my eyes all alone.

I paid the $273 and laid on the table. I screamed as I felt the virtue leave my body. There was no more life in my body and no more life in my soul. I believe that one of the worst things a woman can endure is to lay back and allow someone to kill what God allowed to be a human soul inside of her. I became the shell of a person, and I just wanted to die.

A few days later the guilt of the pain got to me. I grabbed a razor and firmly glided the blade across my wrist. I didn't cut deep enough to tell or to die. It was, however, enough for me recognize that I was lost. I also admitted to myself that if I didn't stop attempting to take my life, one would yield success.

These are the things that make me feel ashamed before God and others, but did you know that if God's grace is sufficient for me, it is sufficient for you? God kept me through all of this. I recall these memories because there are other little girls like me. My story mirrors many other broken women walking around chasing the same men in different bodies not recognizing that what they really need is healing and restoration.

Until we know exactly who we are destined to become, we will continue this detrimental cycle. Ironically, Sean came back to me after the damage had already been done to apologize for hitting me, calling me names, humiliating me, and denying the baby. I forgave him, but the baby was gone.

I was hurt for him and for me. Our immaturity caused me to make an irrational decision that resulted in the loss of a life. How immature of me. I was woman enough to lie down and conceive but I wasn't woman enough to give life and instead, I took one.

My anguish and the drinking continued. I drank so much that many times I blacked out and would wake up in places that I had no clue where I was or how I got there or what happened during the time of the black out. I stayed drunk.

There were also fun and amazing moments. In middle school I was on the cheerleading squad. I really enjoyed those fun times. I tried something a little different. I began dating a popular basketball player named Grown Dog, but we didn't have sex.

There was no abuse involved and honestly, I didn't know how to handle that so our relationship didn't last long. The kids at school respected us as a couple and the crew called me Mrs. Grown Dog. Funny, how you can be in an abusive environment for so long that when a healthy relationship comes along you don't know what to do with it. I was still a very angry little girl.

I fought in school a lot of times, and I was quite destructive. I didn't know how to express myself so I was a bitch all the time; real rough around the edges. I was a broken soul. I was suspended from school often and ended up being forced to attend an alternative school.

Ironically this change had a positive affect on me. I was attending 68th Street School, and we had an African American play during Black History Month. I was selected to play Harriet Tubman. This was the first time that I could actually say that I felt honored. I have never forgotten that moment.

At my previous schools I was good at running track and cheerleading but those were all things that brought attention to me. Never had I taken the time to learn or understand the shoes of someone who represented greatness or someone who committed their life to helping others. That feeling has been my motivation since that moment.

The next year I was 15 years old in the 9th grade, and I was pregnant again by another older man. This time I decided to keep the baby. Many would hope that after so many issues and trauma, things could get better but they did not.

Unfortunately, things had taken a turn in a negative direction. During my pregnancy, my grandmother would say, "girl, you don't have a job and you are still in high school, how are you going to take care of a baby?" I received child support from my father, and every month, I would contribute a little money towards a furniture layaway at a nearby store.

By the time the baby was born, the two of us moved into a beautiful low-income apartment with our brand new furniture. I was determined even in the midst of my mess. When I set my mind towards something, I really wanted to accomplish it. At 16, I was a mother with no training and no clue how to create a life for the two of us.

All I knew was that it was my goal to be a better mother than what my mother had been to me. Yet, I didn't have the skills, the love, the training or the desire to mother my son properly. Having a child was not the best decision for me at the time, but I am glad I did. I was the most absent mother ever.

In addition to my mother's abuse I was a latchkey kid. She was in the nursing field so when she was not abusing me, I was left alone. Understanding how that felt, I didn't leave my son at home, but I would drop him off every chance I got. He spent a lot of time at my mother's house, with friends, and at his Godmother's home.

Most weekends and many weeknights, my son was with someone else. I ran the streets because I didn't have time for a child. I was a child myself. When he was born, I didn't even have sense enough to hold my baby. As he grew up, I was often reminded of this because he and I were so different from each other.

We had an arrangement; I fed, clothed, and took care of him and he, well, he was just there. My son had a tough beginning. His father wasn't around, and I was a kid raising a kid. I am glad that he at least survived my cooking, if that's what you want to call it. In addition to the babysitter, the TV also bought me time.

I just sat him in front of the screen hoping he would learn the basics of life.

He was the cutest baby ever, and he didn't cry much. He loved cars, toys and just being a boy. However, as he began growing and coming into his own, his cute disposition was only witnessed while he was around me.

He fought and got in trouble at school as early as age 3. The schools would call me often about his behavior. Not only did I begin to get agitated from their calls but I was also tired of them calling to notify me. I didn't know any better so I blamed all of his poor behavior on him.

What do hurt people do? They hurt people. I was a poor excuse for a mother. And even though my son was beyond handsome, the pain behind his eyes was evident. It was as if I had transferred my hurt and disappointment over to him. He was also deeply saddened because his father wasn't in his life.

I recall a time when I dropped him off at school, and I watched him walk towards the playground. He looked down at the ground as he walked. Nothing bad happened that morning, he was just painted with sorror.

He didn't have many friends because he had fought them all. It was at that moment that I realized that something wasn't right with him, and he was missing some key elements in his young life. I just wasn't smart enough to know what he needed or wanted to heal the hole in his heart.

## *-Love Hurts-*

*This type of love hurts. I was ok with it at first. My only thirst was to be his first love. I ended up becoming a victim of his "fist" love. You see it never occurred to me that it would be me; the one wanting to be free. But who would listen to me?*

*God's word says that HE was there in the beginning and the end but who was there when I couldn't even hold a pen? They say it takes 8 times, I said they say it takes 8 times before I WILL really leave him, but really leave him? How do I really leave him?*

*Would you really leave him? And go where?*

*Do you see the pain in my eyes? Listen to the words from my mouth. Watch how I walk. Pay close attention, I am lonely, isolated, and made to feel lower than low. But wait baby girl, there is a way that is better than this. It's called freedom. Forgiveness and forever.*

# CHAPTER FIVE:
## *The Saga Continues*

I dropped out of high school and began working at the Fred Astaire dance studio as a telemarketer. I was good at it. This was the first time I started to believe that I could be and do more with my life. My parenting skills were still horrible. My son continued getting in trouble at school, and that really upset me.

As a matter of fact I stayed that way towards him for years. I spent my time anticipating when he would get in trouble again, never considering that my dysfunction required him to deal with issues that caused him trauma as well. I tried disciplining him the only way I knew how. He stayed on extended punishment and was often physically punished. He was acting out so much that he missed many functions with friends and family. As an unfulfilled mother, I had nothing inside to give to him.

My life was spinning out of control with no end. I needed a new mask, and I felt like the mask of money would make all the pain go away. I would be able to provide the things that my son needed financially, and I believed that life would be gravy.

One day a friend mentioned a program called Professional Receptionist Institute. It was a program that received funds from a private source to help young mothers learn about becoming a professional receptionist.

The program lasted for about 6 weeks, and the students learned the basics of Microsoft Office, customer service, professional dress, interviewing techniques and how to represent a professional company as the frontline employee. Professionals in this capacity were also known as the gate keepers. At the end of the program, the graduates had the opportunity to engage in an internship at a prestigious company.

I enrolled in the program and attended during the day and worked at the Fred Astaire Dance Studio at night. Even so, this was not enough money, and the pressure of being a single mother continued to get the best of me. I had a couple of friends making money hand over fist, and I was making peanuts. I knew that if I would just learn the ropes I too could make all this go away and at least make my son happy.

I was an ambitious woman. Although I did not finish my high school education, I knew that one day I would accomplish that goal. However, at this time I was 17 years old and living on my own with a young child to care for. My job as a receptionist paid me only $8.50 per hour. I began to receive coaching on how to become a stripper and all of the perks, warnings, parties, special dates, drugs and of course my favorite, alcohol. Once training was complete, I began traveling as a dancer.

On the weekends and vacation time off work, I would travel to Indiana, Missouri, Maryland and DC to make money. I was one of the blessed ones, and I was able to hide my second life from my family and many of my friends. I would fly out Friday after work and would return no later than Monday morning on a 6am flight just in time for work.

At this time, I was in a long term relationship and even my boyfriend did not know what I was doing. One day, he found a picture of me and a girl that led him to believe that I was in a relationship with a woman. I informed him that I was not in a relationship with a woman and that I had no interest in a relationship of that nature. It was hard for me to explain, hard for him to understand and hard for us to continue being together.

He had a daughter whom I loved and cared for when we were together. I simply brushed it off and told him I just had wild friends. He had no clue that I was not as innocent as I appeared to be.

Nonetheless, the relationship ended and a new one began.

When my relationship ended with him, I was on to the next guy. He had no clue either. I was completely torn inside. I was Rhonda by day and Brittany by night. This conflict became a way of life for me. I also knew that if my family ever found out, they would never understand what I was doing. I can remember the DJ would ask what song I would like played while on stage?

One of my favorite songs at the time was Sweet Potato Pie by Domino. Every time it was my turn to grace the stage, the DJ would play that song and it became my theme song. To this day, I can't stand that song as it reminds me of such a bad time in my life.

Many types of guys came to the club ranging from the innocent young bachelor celebrating his last night of his freedom, to the married creep looking to fulfill his fantasy that was never satisfied at home and hustlers looking to make it rain.

The club also had its share of celebrities who would come in to show off. In our world it was all about getting booked for an after party performance. This is where you make the real money.

The guys looking for something after the club would scope out the women like they were at a meat market.

When not on stage, girls would walk around the club making love with their eyes until they were selected for the next party. These practices were often serious safety hazards because some girls didn't make it home the next day. I was pretty young so I had the privilege of the insight from my friends and the vets in the business. They would tell me who was ok to go with and who was not. I stayed drunk during this time.

One day something changed for me. I became aware of something greater than myself. At the club, we had what was called a "house mom". Her job was to sell exotic dancewear. One night, she happened to be reading a book and while she was reading, I ask her what she was reading? She responded, "the Quran." She went on to speak about how she used to be like each of us and that she wasn't there to change anyone. She expressed that she was only there to provide us with an option should we seek it. Her reasoning for being there was to sell us as exotic dancers. While she was reading I began to cry. It wasn't that I wanted to become a Muslim but this was the first time that I realized that there was a God that was watching my actions and was not pleased with my behavior.

It was the first time I connected with the thought of God and his existence. It was at this moment that all the pain I was feeling came rushing back.

Everything that I was trying to bury, hide, forget, and let go, all came back at one time.

I was embarrassed by my existence, my appearance, and by the seeds that I had sown in my life. I felt completely degraded and the truth of the matter is that I had done it to myself. There were women who had pimps, and young girls who had lost their lives in this night scene.

One day I woke up at a house with a guy that I had seen several times and yet this time, he was doing heroin. This freaked me out because my drug of choice was alcohol and marijuana, every now and then. I was afraid by the mere thought that I could be in a dangerous situation.

Heroin is a drug that is not to be played with. We all have heard of the horror stories behind heroin. Thankfully I played it safe and made it out. God's grace was with me the entire time I was so deeply involved in this life. There were so many times that I was so under the influence that I could have easily become a victim of more abuse and even death but glory to God, I wasn't.

One day I went to a family dinner with a friend and right before we ate, we all made a circle holding hands, and a gentleman by the name of Marlon began to pray. I had never experienced that before.

In that moment, I felt something strange but this time, I was able to identify what that feeling was. Once again I was moved to tears and the sadness filled my heart.

That feeling was the amazing presence of God. I was truly overwhelmed and unable to explain my encounter with any one. At the end of the prayer Marlon invited everyone to church. I was simply curious. God was calling me and I just didn't know it.

## *Frame Your World With Your Words*

**REPEAT:**

*I can hear therefore I listen, and I obey.*

*I Am Not That Fabulous*

*The room is closing in. The darkness of my existence is calling me louder than ever and so my subconscious speaks. I am not that fabulous.*

*The more I try, the more I am pulled back in.*

*The fear of freedom reminds me that I am not that fabulous. You must go on.*

*Smile and make apparent moves to keep yourself from dropping the mask.*

*I am not that fabulous.*

*Waiting to live or waiting to die. Waiting to exhale and fly.*

*I am in the midst of myself my and alone.*

*Yet I think to myself,*

*I am not that fabulous.*

*Not that fabulous the voices say, you are not that fabulous. Fearful, astonishing you are, because you love others unconditionally you shall not lose.*

*Being able to break free from the thoughts that haunt me, the thoughts that shame me, the thoughts that imprisoned me.*

*I know yes, yes, yes I know.*

*You would say I am not that fabulous.*

*But contrary my dear I am:*

- *Fearless*
- *Amazing*
- *Beautiful*
- *Unconditionally flawed*
- *Loyal to a degree of crazy understanding*
- *Outrageously bold*
- *Unapologetic for my existence*
- *Scientifically PROVEN to be the best creation God made for man yet not to be taken by man.*

*I am a fabulous woman. Fabulous is me.*

# CHAPTER SIX:

*Found By The King*

In prayer, standing hand in hand in a circle joined with others, I heard a voice say "you have tried everything else in life, why not give God a try?" In that moment, I was reminded of the feeling I had in the night club where the house mom was reading her Quran. I was reminded that God existed, and he was more than just an option for me. He was my answer.

My self-worth was so low and I was so lost, yet I had no clue how to fix my life. The show Iyanla Fix My Life wasn't available back then, so I had to figure it out and I eventually did, at the alter.

The following Sunday, January 27, 1997 with a man laying in my bed, I rushed out the house to acceot Marlon's invitation to attend church.

I needed to be touched in my soul and I now recognized that the only way I would ever experience that feeling was in the presence of God. I had already experienced his presence, and now I wanted to get to know him.

At the end of service, the pastor asked for those in need of prayer to come to the alter. I wasn't a praying person at all and didn't even know or understand the benefits of prayer, church or a relationship with God. However, there was something drawing me near. I now know this drawing as the spirit of God.

God is a spirit and those that worship him must do so in spirit and in truth. When I went to the alter for prayer, I felt completely washed and cleaned. It was as if I were being renewed and transitioned into a new life. I confessed to God with my words, my heart, and my soul that I was a sinner and that I believed God raised Christ from the grave on the 3rd day.

That was it. I was born again! I remembered my grandmother telling me of God's glory as a little girl but I allowed the hurt of my past to take me down a destructive path.

For 3 days after washing away my sins, I didn't speak to anyone. My tongue felt heavy and words were far few and in between. By the 4th day, I was a completely different person. When others spoke to me using profanity, it bothered me. I was no longer using profane language myself. Weird huh?

That alone let me know that something had really happened to me that changed me deep inside of my core.

I began to read the Bible as many hours as I could every day, and I spent at least 2 hours in prayer every day after work.

My heart, mind, and soul had been cleansed. I began to believe what the Bible said about me. I went to church faithfully twice a week for the next 15 years and never returned to my old ways again.

I didn't know the plans that God had for me to prosper and to give me hope and an expected end. He was creating a true **BOSS (Built Out of Survival Situations)** in me. I learned that I was built from survival. For me, building self-worth also meant comprehending who Christ was in me. If I were to continue to grow, I had to be aware that he was now in me. I valued the sacrifice of Jesus on the cross; therefore, I too am resurrected in him.

My soul had been crying out for help, and I didn't even know it. There was light at the end of the tunnel for me, and there was an eternal promise given to me that day at the alter. Like many who walked that long walk to the alter, I surrendered to the spirit of God.

Falling in love with Jesus was the first time I felt free. The process of healing for some can take many years, but I trusted the process and the journey has brought me such joy.

A black cloud hovered over me my entire life. On January 27, 1997, that black cloud was broken.

My purpose on earth was beginning to be revealed to me. And although I had a long journey ahead of me, I didn't care how long it was going to take. I was so happy to have been found by the one who created me, and the one who knew me, and who loved me. God's love is just that amazing.

In addition to learning about God, I would spend hours everyday discovering my purpose and how God could one day use me. I now believe that God caught all the tears that I shed and placed them in a jar to later pour them on me with love at the appointed time.

In his presence, I had the fullness of joy. I have since had many encounters with God, and I know without question that what he did for me, he can do for you.

I became a worshipper of God. In doing so, I realized that praise is amazing but worship is how you can truly get intimate with God. There were times when I was in prayer and God would remind me of the times that he was right by my side.

Even in the night club while drinking and being some man's fantasy, God would open my eyes to show me how many times he protected me from harm. I often cried for months. I couldn't understand why such a pure Holy being would see me as special.

The spirit of God convinced me that my life mattered to him and even with my shame, there is purpose. WOW! I am still amazed by this love. God is love. There is nothing like the love of God because it covers all things. I was covered in the midst of overdose, abuse, sin, addiction, sickness and unforgiveness. God's love covers all.

There is nothing too hard for him. Sometimes people get mad at God because they don't understand why he allowed things to happen in their lives. Instead of questioning him, we must learn to thank him for allowing us to survive.

We must remember that there is a purpose greater than each of us. Now that I have been found by the King and understand his love, I cannot imagine my life without his love. There is no love without

God because God is love. God offers us favor for our souls, reprieve from our hurt, and grace for our sins. There is room for you too at the cross. All of our sins, disappointments, burdens, shortcomings, and, faults have been paid for by Jesus Christ on the cross.

Upon my new awakening, I was granted a second chance at life. I now have the tools necessary to make a difference in my life and the lives of those I come in contact with. In the end, I win. Sickness, sin, abuse and even addictions could not separate me from the love of God.

The Bible speaks to this in Romans 8: 31-39:

31 What shall we say about such wonderful things as these? If God is for us, who can ever be against us?

32 Since he did not spare even his own Son but gave him up for us all, won't he also give us everything else?

33 Who dares accuse us whom God has chosen for his own? No one—for God himself has given us right standing with himself.

34 Who then will condemn us? No one— for Christ Jesus died for us and was raised to life for us, and he is sitting in

the place of honor at God's right hand, pleading for us.

35 Can anything ever separate us from Christ's love? Does it mean he no longer loves us if we have trouble or calamity, or are persecuted, or hungry, or destitute, or in danger, or threatened with death?

36 (As the Scriptures say, "For your sake we are killed every day; we are being slaughtered like sheep."[a])

37 No, despite all these things, overwhelming victory is ours through Christ, who loved us.

38 And I am convinced that nothing can ever separate us from God's love. Neither death nor life, neither angels nor demons,[b] neither our fears for today nor our worries about tomorrow—not even the powers of hell can separate us from God's love.

> 39 No power in the sky above or in the earth below—indeed, nothing in all creation will ever be able to separate us from the love of God that is revealed in Christ Jesus our Lord.

Becoming a Christian does not mean that you automatically become immune to life. I still had more life to live and more experience to endure. I went on to live through two failed marriages and at times found myself in the midst of sadness, but I knew that this time around, I did not have to walk this life alone.

The more I grow the more I know that my faith is the guiding force for my life. Without God in my life, I could easily be back in the mental hospital because life had become too heavy of a burden.

Even today, I experience challenges and struggles just like everyone else, but this time I have the power to not be overtaken. I have the power of words to frame my world. I am still a fighter but today, I fight with my words, and I fight in the spirit through prayer.

## *Frame your World with Your Words*

### REPEAT:

*God is the author and finisher of my faith.*

## *Inspirational IV*

*Don't run from pain.*

*This is the time when endurance is developed and through the pressure a diamond is revealed.*

*Embrace every thing life has to offer*

*and when you subdue and conquer your hurt, out of the ground you rise!*

*Stronger and better than ever, your best days are ahead of you, not behind.*

# CHAPTER SEVEN:

*The Recovery*

**Steps for a Successful Recovery**

Becoming a born again believer does not mean life is going to be perfect, but it does mean that you don't have to do it alone.

**Step One: Repentance & Forgiveness**

The process for God to choose me and for me to accept the call started with me repenting and acknowledging that I had sin and had fallen short of his glory. I asked God to forgive me of all my sins and for causing so much additional damage to myself. With a simple prayer, he forgave me.

I quickly learned that God's forgiveness wasn't the only forgiveness that I needed. I had to also forgive myself. How do I do that? How do I even learn about myself enough to recognize the best version of me?

What does all this forgiveness mean? I was unchurched and was completely out of touch with the healing and restoration process.

Once I learned how to silence my own voice, I began to listen to my heart that spoke of how to forgive myself and others.

**Matthew 6:14**

*For if you forgive other people when they sin against you, your heavenly Father will also forgive you.*

This is something that I have continued to carry with me. I am not saying that I haven't messed up here and there but it is my heart's desire to forgive those that wronged me as fast as humanly possible.

**Step Two: Cleanse**

The moment that I understood that what happened to me was not my fault was monumental. Even with the substance abuse, the promiscuous behavior and every other sin that haunted me, I learned to recognize that I was made whole with Christ.

> **2 Corinthians 5:17**
>
> *Therefore, if anyone is in Christ, he is a new creation. The old has passed away; behold, the new has come.*

I was a new creation and therefore all that happened before that moment was washed away under the forgiveness of Jesus Christ our Lord.

**Step Three: Study**

Not only did I surrounded myself with strong leaders such as Pastor Melva Henderson, Pastor

Pamela Hines, Pastor Dana World Patterson, Cleopatra White, Krislynn World, Mother Tucker, and my Godmother, Felicia Washington, but I also allowed them to encircle me with their positive energy.

They were always praying for me, giving me advice, providing me with structure, guidance, and most importantly love. Through their non judgmental love, they taught me the word of God and raised me to be strong and proud of who I was. Having a winning circle was crucial for my deliverance.

My gifts started to flourish and grow. My journey towards faith is what makes me as unique as my DNA. I also wanted to get involved with my church right away. I stayed very busy for the first seven years of deliverance.

I started out praying for the youth at the youth detention center, and then I prayed for others at the alter when they were coming into their faith for the first time. We called this "alter ministry". Later, I returned to my first love, dance.

I originally thought I would never dance again; my gift had been so tarnished with poor choices, but I was wrong. Our church was one of the largest African American churches in the state of Wisconsin, and we had a dance group. We referred to our style of dance as "praise dancing". I joined the dance team and for 4 years I danced, learned, and trained. I had no idea that God was preparing me to be a director of dance.

I began the first children's dance ministry in my church with over 43 dancers ranging from 3 to 13 years of age. Another level of accountability was upon me, so I took a minister's class at my church that lasted for over a year, and I became a licensed minister.

This was the most accomplished that I had ever felt in my life. Many of the people that I ministered to didn't even know how broken and shattered I was or how much helping others was so far from my original plans for myself.

**Step Four: Speak Life**

Now that I understood the heart of forgiveness, I now had to learn to change my language and the way in which I spoke about myself. My old Pastors Skip and Melva Henderson taught me to frame my world with my words. This has been my motto and fortress for many years. I have learned the art of speaking my reality. I encourage you to do the same.

You can change your reality with the words that come out of your mouth. I am not saying that everything will be perfect, but your words and belief in the world you set for them will change your perspective on life and your circumstance. Pastor Skip used to always say "Faith is a muscle."

He meant that faith is practice and with practice comes perfection. For example, it's hard to believe that God will heal you of Cancer when you didn't practice believing in his healing from a headache. Using your voice is one sure way to reframe your reality. Doing so creates confidence, builds faith, and changes your perspective.

## Matthew 11:23-25

*23 I tell you the truth, you can say to this mountain, 'May you be lifted up and thrown into the sea,' and it will happen. But you must really believe it will happen and have no doubt in your heart. 24 I tell you, you can pray for anything, and if you believe that you've received it, it will be yours. 25 But when you are praying, first forgive anyone you are holding a grudge against, so that your Father in heaven will forgive your sins, too.*

**Step Five: Giving**

Today, giving is the new normal for me. My journey embodies the essence of selflessness and being my sister's keeper. I wish I could tell you that I passed every test and that I no longer made poor choices or had bouts of depression and low self-esteem but I can't. However, God still has favored me. I still win with Him.

After being restored, I now experienced making better choices. This time, I knew my value. I was also aware of what I wasn't going to tolerate which included abusive men.

**Step Six: Knowing What You Want**

Knowing what you want is one of the most mature accomplishments we can make as an adult. Do you recall being in school and being asked what you wanted to be when you grew up?

As a child I didn't know how important that question was and more importantly, I never knew the answer. There were two things that I do remember saying. I remember stating that I wanted to be a counselor and a model.

How ironic that my life has led me back to a role in which I would serve as a counselor to others through ministry. This was God's plan for me. I needed to be cultivated and molded into really knowing not only what I wanted to be when I grew up but my purpose. I was created to be a voice for those that don't have a voice and for those who are afraid to speak.

**Step Seven: No Excuses**

You must deliberately work on your gifts with no excuses. It took a long time for me to really recognize my purpose. Pastor Melva Henderson used to teach us that time spent in preparation is never wasted.

**Step Eight: Upgrade Your Value**

Upgrading my value with education and a winning circle was key. I was never a model student. I skipped school and slept during class most days. Somehow with only a General Education Diploma (GED), I wanted to become an entrepreneur.

I was recruited for a position at a company as an assistant property manager. I held that position for about 3 years, and during that time, my manager thought I was beginning to lack motivation.

My manager sent me to a real estate seminar, and the main speaker was Zig Ziglar.

This seminar was a blessing and a curse for me. I was blessed listening to Zig Ziglar as I reflected on my life and the goals that I desired to accomplish. After so many struggles, I decided to embrace entrepreneurship in the area of real estate.

The curse would be that my supervisor would lose an employee. I began working as an Assistant Property Manager in the last quarter of my job.

Zig Ziglar said, "Every day that you go to work, make it one more day that you are closer to your dreams." My dreams included doing something that no one in my family had ever done.

My grandparents owned rental property, but I wanted to take my business to the next level. Zig Ziglar encouraged the students to have at least 8 streams of income and not rely on a job. He used "Just Over Broke" as an acronym for job.

My passion for real estate grew so fast within a couple years. I had obtained enough real estate that I no longer had to work for anyone. I realized back then that entrepreneurship was not for everyone, but I did not have anything to lose.

I also opened a childcare business named Rhonda's Reading Rainbow while I earned my real estate licensing. I was in the millionaire club the first year in the business, and I went on to become a real estate investor.

In the midst of all of that success, the recession impacted me just as it did for millions of other Americans, and my investment property plummeted.

I relocated to Atlanta, GA and felt that I wanted to continue in business for myself, but I wanted to expand my circle and my net worth. A higher education was necessary for the next phase of life.

After receiving my Bachelor's in Business Management, I started to feel that I was on a new path of accountability for myself. I refined my speaking and presentation skills and gained more insight as to how the business world operated.

My circle changed very quickly and the amazing ladies that I shared common interests with reminded me of the amazing women from my hometown who had taken me under their wings. This time I had more to contribute versus others always pouring into me.

It is crucial to invest in your craft and surround yourself with friends that inspire you to become better than you have been.

My faith grew stronger. My spiritual awareness manifested, and as I began learning about God, I wanted to help people. It made a big difference in my life and made me into a woman.

While my career excelled, so did my finances, family, and forgiveness for those that hurt me in the past. At the closing of my real estate and childcare business, I successfully grossed over a 6 figure income.

**Step Nine: Know Your Reason Why**

I am now a mature forty year old mom, student of life, minister, and business woman. My journey was for a reason. Overcoming the many obstacles in my path has made me the woman I am today. I am still becoming. I have also decided to commit the rest of my life to helping abused women and children by opening a non-profit organization named Rose of Sharon Transitional Living for Women Inc.

My organization cultivates women and children from broken foundations and works to restore hope by providing services to meet their needs. I thank God for my faith, friends, and family who cheered me on all the way through this journey. This is how I became the woman I am from the inside out.

As I reflect on where I come from and the hurt that I endured, I am also reminded that not every man was bad to me. I dated a guy who was 18 years my senior. He had no clue about the turmoil that I lived with everyday but he was always an inspiration to me.

He loved me through my pain, but I just didn't know how to receive that love. He taught me a lot and assisted in the woman that I became. My reason, my why, my destiny is not for me but the legacy that I will leave behind. I will leave a mark on this earth to let the world know that I was here.

**Step Ten: Sow Seeds**

Sow the seeds that you want to reap. Some may even call it karma. When making a decision that will affect someone else, we must be unselfish. We all have been selfish at some point or another. The first law of nature is self-preservation. What's that? It is simply to be selfish.

On the airplane the flight attendant advises the passengers to secure their own mask before helping someone else. At that time you must be selfish and protect your own life first. It is unrealistic to ask others to not be selfish.

However, if you want to reap seeds of a great harvest, you must be willing to unselfishly sow into someone else's life.

Support someone else's vision and yours will evolve right before your eyes. Learn to be faithful to God and the leadership he has given you. If you don't have a leader, I suggest you find one. Serving someone else is a sure way to not only reap, but it also trains you in the interim.

On the contrary, you can sow seeds of damnation unto yourself by the choices you make. The unspoken laws of life govern the process of sowing and reaping. If you plant an apple seed, you won't reap an orange tree. You reap exactly what you sow.

If you are sowing on fertile ground, there are times that you have to water your seeds and take out the weeds as well. You are the gardener of your own garden. You create the harvest you want to eat from.

### Gal 6:7

*Do not be deceived: God cannot be mocked.* A man reaps what he sows.

# CHAPTER EIGHT:
*Life After Abuse*

Even as you have read my personal story, I still feel compelled to teach anyone who will listen to not only recognize the signs of abuse but to also advocate for friends, family, and loved ones. It is possible that one day, the life you save may be your own.

Abuse comes in many forms and often goes unnoticed because there is not any physical evidence. Abuse can be physical, financial, emotional, sexual or verbal. Even if you have not experienced physical abuse, you may have encountered verbal abuse from a partner, family member or fellow co-worker.

If so, can you remember how it made you feel? Did it shape your perception of yourself or others? Of course it did in some shape, form or fashion.

Please note, we can even be our own abuser. We abuse ourselves everyday with addictions and self-inflicted pain. In this chapter, I share the Cycle of Abuse. I believe that when a victim can admit and recognize that she is in a cycle, then and only then will she realize that the abuse will continue.

If we can identify the cycle, the light bulb comes on, and we are now looking out for it. I like to use the analogy of a horse wearing blinders. When the horse is wearing blinders, he is focused on what is ahead; therefore, he is not fearful of the things on either side of him because he doesn't see them.

An abusive relationship is similar. When the we are able to remove the blinders, we can see the real danger that we are in. Survival is more important than maintaining the toxic relationship.

## *Signs of Abuse*

Recognizing an abusive relationship early on is one of the best forms of protection. One early sign of abuse is fear of your partner. You could also observe this same fear in others. You may be fearful even in the midst of conversation. If the conversation doesn't go the partner's way, he or she may blow up, and make you feel as if you have to walk on eggshells.

Other warning signs include: limiting access to money, displaying jealous behavior, isolation, humiliation, forced sex, and blame.

Violence towards pets or children and short tempers toward service personal are also behaviors to monitor.

Pay close attention when threats and verbal abuse are present as they can often lead to violence.

If you or anyone you know is experiencing any of these signs, be careful. Domestic violence can also result in murder or suicide.

## *The Cycle of Abuse*

The cycle of abuse is a social cycle theory developed in 1979 by Lenore E. Walker to explain patterns of behavior in an abusive relationship. It should also be noted that grief is a major factor to consider while reclaiming your voice after abuse.

There are 6 stages of grief that you will go through in choosing to over come abuse.

**Stage One – Disbelief**
You begin to struggle with the fact that you were abused, or in an abusive relationship. You also realize that the 'sociopath' or 'psychopath' is not who you thought he would be.

**Stage Two – The Fog of Confusion**
In this stage, you are so confused. You don't want it to be true. The abuser can be charming, and when everything is good, it's really good. This can't be! Be careful, because this is when you can be lured back into the relationship, and the cycle will start over again.

**Stage Three – Heartache, Depression and Sadness**
You are embarrassed; your heart is aching, and yet the reality hits you like a ton of bricks. You are now faced with the choice to leave or stay.

**Stage Four – Isolation and Emptiness**
When you are feeling alone, who can you tell? At this stage, you may have lost something valuable to you, such as your job, friends or family.

**Stage Five – Psychological Detective**
In this phase, you may begin to become over zealous about research to help you figure out what you are dealing with, and may decide to seek relationship

counseling. It can help. Couples counseling is never recommended for an abusive relationship. The abuser needs anger management and specialized therapy.

**Stage Six – Acceptance, Healing and Recovery**
Once you have accepted the progression of events, you start to focus on getting back to you and possibly an even better version of yourself. Your self-worth is discovered again and you are free. As a survivor, you realize that you matter and that you are worth more than what you have endured.

Understanding your self-worth is the beginning of a new future. There is a grief process that comes with ending anything, even moreso, with ending a toxic relationship. This is mainly because the victim never wanted the relationship to end, only the abuse. It's as if someone ripped off a bandage on the skin where a scar had begun to heal and now the wound is exposed.

It can feel like someone ripped your heart out of your chest, and it was beating in their hands while you bled to death. The victim ultimately wanted the relationship to survive and thrive, but in the end, he or she is left with broken pieces. If children are involved, the victim is looking at the children with pain in their eyes trying to understand how to put life back together again. I am here to tell you that there is hope!

For me, it was understanding that I deserved better and that I would not tolerate anyone abusing me any longer.

I became very angry with most men even if they did no wrong. Was that the right method to begin healing? Absolutely not!

As a matter of fact that made matters worse for me. Not only was I dealing with my own insecurities, now I created a toxic relationship where there was no need. Hurt people; hurt people.

Finding my faith in God has been my true source of healing and deliverance. I hope that will be the same for you. In order to have life after abuse; one must live.

The victim must be free from abuse. He or she must get out of the relationship. Couples or marriage counseling won't fix an abuser. The abuser must seek professional, individual anger management counseling. In the meantime the victim must be completely safe and secure away from the abuser.

Statistics have shown that the victim is in more extreme danger of death when fleeing an abuser; therefore, a calculated escape plan must be created to protect the life of the victim when she decides to leave the relationship. My suggestion is to contact the local domestic violence agency in the area where the victim lives or the national domestic violence hotline. Additionally, it would be wise to explain the situation so they can assist with creating a plan that fits each victim.

There is not a one size fits all plan. Everyone's circumstances are different; therefore, a customized plan is what's needed to ensure the safety of all involved.

Once the abuser realizes that the victim has left the relationship, he or she will begin looking for that victim. The abuser's anger will be fierce when a victim finally decides to leave. This message is translated into the victim taking back control over his or her life and saying to the abuser "You no longer can control me". (See sample escape plan at the end of this chapter.)

On average, it is said that survivors will leave the abuser a total of 8 times before leaving for good or worst being murdered. While fleeing, the survivor may feel the need to call the abuser for whatever reason. It could be for the need of money or to update him or her on the status of the children.

During this conversation, the abuser will often encourage the survivor that he or she is sorry, it won't happen again, I love you, and we can work this out. Another line abusers often use is "I will get help" or "I want my family together." When the survivor refuses to comply, additional threats are made like, "I am going to find you, and when I do, I will kill you or "I am going to kill your family."

Take these threats seriously and stay away. Make sure a temporary restraining order is in place. A piece of paper cannot stop a bullet or someone from violating the law, but it will assist the law in intervening when necessary. A temporary restraining order can be granted and be used as evidence in court when its time to persue charges.

Once the survivor has gotten in a secure location and some time has lapsed, then the healing process is starting to set in. As long as he or she is in a thriving environment that promotes faith, love, support and encouragement, this survivor will began to get strong again. He or she will began to realize the value that is within and will start the process of changing her mind set.

Returning to a toxic environment that resembles that of abuse, lack, drugs, alcohol etc. will only perpetuate a continued cycle of abuse. What I am saying is the survivor not only needs to flee an abuser but also consider the environment that made abuse acceptable.

Many times victims are in abusive relationships because they are a product of their environment. Seeing abuse in the home as a child or knowing friends that are in physically abusive relationships contribute to such exposure.

This type of environment speak volumes to a victim. This tells victims that everyone is doing it. Many question ask the question: who will want me once I leave? When you leave you may also hear that you have to return because this is just what your mother and grandmother went through and that it will all work out in time.

Domestic violence is NOT ok! It is wrong and it is a crime! Domestic violence is more than just a slap or push. Many women everyday loose their lives due to this horrendous crime. Their children are left to figure out how to live without mommy and daddy because now daddy is in jail.

In the state of Georgia according to the 2015 Fatality Review Report from 2010-2014 more than 62,000 children were on the scene of a domestic violence incident, and in 2015, 139 familicide cases were reported which was the highest in ten years.

It has also been reported that in 47% of domestic violence cases, survivors and abusers share children and during custody exchange, the violence continues.

With news like this, it is vital to have a strategic escape plan if children are involved. It is crucial to continue with a safety plan for times of sharing custody, school and extended family functions.

Now that a safety plan is in place for leaving and staying away; rebuilding from the inside out is huge.

Get involved with the local church, synagogue, mosque, temple or wherever you worship.

My belief is in Christianity. Jesus Christ is the way, the truth and the light. No one comes to the father except by the son. I am sensitive to the fact that many readers may have another faith base for their life. Ones belief in God is the only way to keep you on track and to remain faithful to making healthy, relationship choices.

One point I want to make, have you noticed that I used the term victim and survivor interchangeably? This is because a victim must be free from the abuse to become a survivor. Outside of being a survivor, he or she may feel compelled to reach back and help someone else. This qualifies him or her as an overcomer.

An overcomer is one that has surpassed survival and is now an advocate of some kind. A voice for the voiceless! This person finds strength in seeing others find their voice again. This is not everyone's story, but it is for me.

Life doesn't come with an instruction book; however, experience in the life of others is supposed to be used as a guide to help us get the picture.

Life after abuse is tricky for each person. This is why I encourage a total change of environment, especially if the current circumstance supported violence of any kind. Once I decided to change my environment, that is when I began to live life the way it was intended to be.

We must evolve from abuse to abundance. You could never have told me that I would be a vessel used by God to make a difference in this lifetime. I would never have believed that I would be a voice for the voiceless.

It would have been completely unbelieveable for you to have told me that I would have graduated from college with almost a 4.0 grade point average and that my voice would be heard globally.

Because I am an overcomer, I survived, I won! Guess what, you are a winner too! There is something great in store for you. You may not have suffered abuse, but you know someone who has. Someone you love and care about and you can be a voice for them.

Because domestic violence is your business, you can no longer turn a blind eye and say the traditional statement "Why won't she just leave?" Remove the judgment from yourself and others. I just don't believe that abusers want to abuse.

They need help as survivors need help, and together we can save our families by being that community that truly fight the good fight together. If you know of an abuser, find help for them. If you know a survivor don't judge her for not leaving when you think its bad!

The truth of the matter is that it's been bad before you found out. By the time you find out, it could be too late. Help give life to those that may feel that they are loosing theirs. Many times we can be a lifeline to someone that is weak. There are many reasons a victim may not leave an abuser, we are not here to judge; yes, we want this to stop now and want the victim to get to safety, however, support and love will help them to see that love doesn't hurt.

Love is an action that is pain free and feels good. Without that love or support, victims feel stuck. They feel as though no one will understand or help them.

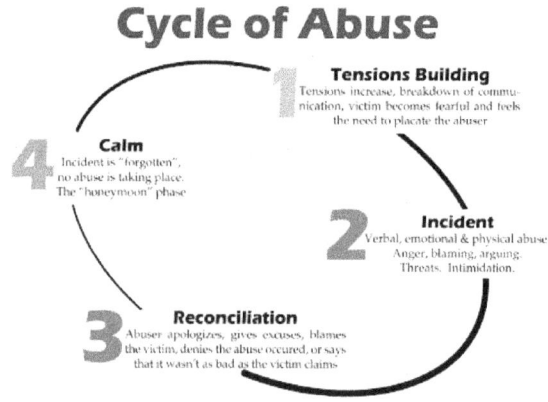

## *Ten Easy Steps to Abundant Life:*

1. Forgive yourself and others.
2. Develop a relationship with Christ.
3. Be a giver of life, knowledge and wealth.
4. Above all, choose to love yourself first.
5. Create healthy relationships by trusting until given reason not to.
6. Challenge yourself to achieve the impossible that only God can make possible.
7. Walk in peace.
8. Conquer your fears.
9. Embrace wisdom.
10. Frame your world with your words (speak life).

I have known both success and failure, and I have made many poor decisions, but through it all, I love myself. I love the good, the bad, and the indifferent. This is my journey from abuse to abundance.

## *Frame Your World With Your Words*

**REPEAT:**

*I live a full life in abundance, to the full until now it overflows, I have more than enough love, life, money and health to share.*

## *What areas must I Create Abundant Life for myself?*

**Help a friend with understanding**

Often times outsiders will judge a victim and make comments like, "why doesn't she just leave?" First remove any judgment about the victim and help her when she is ready.

She is afraid and possibly at a heightened risk of death without a calculated escape plan and the help of her family, friends, law enforcement and community.

An escape plan is not a one size fits all. One must be created based on the victim's current situation. Children add another dynamic to consider as well as if the victim has a professional career, is enrolled in school, is a public figure or is an owner of a flourishing business.

Ensuring the safety of the family while leaving the relationship can be successful with the help of a trained domestic violence advocate and/or law enforcement.

A protection order should always be one of the first tasks a victim tackles in this process. In this world of technology, be mindful of the use of cell phones, computers, internet and social media that can be used to track the victim. It should be noted that technology also allows a victim to have a world of information at her finger tips when planning to escape the abuser can be very cunning on watching her every move.

Below and on the next page is a sample escape plan. It gives an idea of what to consider. Be cautious, this is NOT to be used without considering every probable scenario.

## *Sample Escape Plan*

**During violence**

Practice how to leave. Consider which door, window, stairwell etc.

What time of day is best to leave? Is the abuser at work or asleep?

Who can be trusted to tell about the abuse? Leave money? Consider identification, bus/plane ticket new destination.

Teach the children how to use 911 the correct way.

Victims can anticipate a fight when in the midst of transition.

Move to a place where there is a lower risk of injury (as best as possible try to avoid the bathroom, garage, kitchen, near weapons, or in rooms without access to an outside door).

Create a code word for the children and for those that will help.

## *Safety Plan When Leaving*

Leave any important documents and an extra set of car keys with someone.

Increase independence by opening another bank account. Be sure to have the statement emailed instead of being sent to the house.

Clean up social media, internet searches and text messages by deleting any communication that reflects an escape plan.

Contact a shelter and secure a spot to flee to.

If financially feasible, obtain another cell phone and leave it with a trusted friend along with clothes and any other items.

Finally practice the escape plan with the children and trusted friend to ensure accuracy when executing the plan.

## *Frame your world with your words*

**REPEAT:**

*I am my sister's keeper.*

I will be her voice until she can!

## *National Domestic Violence Stats*

1 in 4 women will experience domestic violence in her lifetime. That is more than breast, ovarian and lung cancer combined.

Women ages 18 to 34 are at greatest risk of becoming victims of domestic violence.

More than 4 million women experience physical assault and rape by their partners.

In 2 out of 3 female homicide cases, females are killed by a family member or intimate partner

More than 3 million children witness domestic violence in their homes every year.

Children who live in homes where there is domestic violence also suffer abuse or neglect at high rates (30% to 60%).

Domestic violence victims face high rates of depression, sleep disturbances, anxiety, flashbacks, and other emotional distress

Domestic violence contributes to poor health for many survivors including chronic conditions such as heart disease or gastrointestinal disorders.

Most women brought to emergency rooms due to domestic violence were socially isolated and had few social and financial resources.

Domestic violence costs more than $37 billion a year in law enforcement involvement, legal work, medical and mental health treatment, and lost productivity at companies.

## *Inspirational IV*

*"Sometimes, it feels like you are running on a treadmill and you have increased your speed and efforts but you are not making progress. That's ok. Keep going. You will get stronger."*

Rhonda A. Thompson

# CHAPTER NINE:

*Reclaiming Your Worth*

We all know people that believe wealth is money, and if you don't have it, then that must mean you're poor. You are categorized by your net worth (net worth is the amount by which assets exceed liabilities). I see net worth differently.

Contrary to popular belief, your worth is based on the value you possess, your service, your time and your value for self. Only God will value you more than you or anyone else for that matter. If the highest being of the entire universe will value you more than yourself, why not at least meet him half way?

Now, I am not saying you shouldn't increase your financial net worth or your financial legacy; this is all about restoring one's heart, one's time remaining on earth and one's service to others.

One way to reclaim your worth is removing the mask. We've already talked about steps to take in overcoming abuse to attain abundance; however, people can connect with someone who is relatable and someone who is genuine.

Wearing a mask only creates a false sense of security, and this generates feelings of loneliness and isolation. It concerns me when I hear others say "I don't need anyone." This couldn't be farther from the truth. As a matter of fact, this adds to the false sense of security and isolation.

There is no "I" in team and anyone with a vision or a legacy needs a team of professionals to bring a vision to fruition. Even God uses each of us to bless others. If this is true, why wouldn't we want a true connection with those that we will ultimately need? If you were a philanthropist; you would still need people to give to. Your passion and your cause are what you connect your money to.

In this age of technology, we have become lazy with building relationships and lack true human touch. We are on Facebook, Instagram, and Twitter, and all of the fake reality sites, so we get used to wearing a mask.

I am saying STOP IT! Try being the true version of yourself as often as possible by removing the mask.

People will like the real you better. I am not speaking of make up or weaves, I am merely talking about pretending to be someone you are not, when you are really hurting inside. Trying to keep up with others will keep you in the same place for years to come.

Do I like the finer things in life? Well, of course I do. I have friends that shop daily and buy the latest market finds. That is not my situation, and I don't feel bad if I can't keep up with them. Some of them are as shallow and materialistic as they come.

I also have friends with a real heart of substance and haven't shopped in over a year. That is the friend I call on for advice. I choose to call on friends who is not concerned with the exterior but those concerned with making a difference.

To reclaim your worth, you have to take responsibility for any role that you played in your degradation. Know and understand that your life matters and that there is only one of you. If you are not living life in abundance, then you are living beneath your privileges.

When your life matters to not only you but also others, then you will start to invest in yourself. Investing in yourself is not being selfish, it is to ensure that the brand that you represent is represented in a way that brings honor to your legacy. The brand is you!

Love yourself, take time to get to know you and encourage yourself with investing and creating your environment with love. If Christ is in you, then you are a new creation, and the old is gone.

**2 Corinthians 5:17**

*Therefore, if anyone is in Christ, he is a new creation. The old has passed away; behold, the new has come.*

When a baby is born, the joy we experience is something that cannot be put into words. Everything is new and we are excited to see what this baby can do and what the baby will become. This child can do no wrong to stop us from loving him or her.

As a matter of fact, the more we get to know the baby, the more we begin to love this child.

This is the same way we should love ourselves. Especially for those of us that have a second chance at life and wear the badge of survivor. Some may have survived a divorce, loss of a loved one or chronic illness. This principal applies to us all.

Having a healthy self-worth or self-esteem is crucial in any relationship. Ultimately, this behavior creates a habitat for depression. The cure for this is love. Loving

God helps us to learn to love ourselves again. Through my journey, I learned that with God in me, there is no room for self destructive behaviors or thoughts. Therefore, it is very hard for others to make me into a victim again. By no means am I claiming to have it all together, but I am saying that I now know my value is in Christ, not myself.

With that, I am obligated to love myself even when I don't feel like it or feel as though I deserve it. In addition to forgiving and loving yourself, you also teach others how to treat you. You can accomplish this by setting the standard. For example, I really enjoy event planning and creating over the top experiences for my guests. I have created a reputation of one that spares no expense when creating events.

This has in turn set a standard of expectations for those that celebrate me for special occasions such as my birthday, wedding anniversary, graduation etc. My friends and family think through the process a little more when putting on celebrations for me or I will do it myself. I'm joking but they know what I like and what I believe that I deserve.

This is also true with giving gifts to others. When you give gifts to friends and family for their special occasion, they remember when it's your turn. Even if the gift wasn't expensive, it is the calculated thought that goes into the presentation of that gift. Trust me they recognize and are taking notes on how to treat you at gift time.

With this in mind the same principles apply to your friends and family as it relates to how they speak to you and carry on conversation.

If you don't appreciate profanity, don't use it and don't tolerate it in your presence. Now, you don't have to become the police and tell everyone to stop cursing around you. Your nonverbal communication and how you carry yourself will say it loud and clear. We must allow others to be who they want to be however; if the behavior is directed towards us in a way that reduces the way we feel about ourselves, then we must protect our most viable asset (you).

By modeling to others how you want to be treated, you in turn create a standard of value for those around you regarding you.

Another profound area to address is subordinate fear and guilt.

You have already taken responsibility for your past, poor decisions, you have forgiven yourself, you have acknowledged the love for yourself and for God. In all that, you have the possibility of fear and guilt from not accomplishing what you feel you should have accomplished by this time in life.

You may even experience guilt that you were not in the healthiest place when that certain opportunity came. I am here to tell you that what is for you is for you. Remove the fear and guilt. You are a survivor and whatever will be is going to be. This time it will be bigger and better.

Self-awareness is one of life's most amazing gifts. I can appreciate finding my own errors before someone else. I enjoy the opportunity to have access to a second chance at making things right.

It is quite satisfying to be the first to say "I apologize" and not to hold onto anger or bitterness. Sometimes to apologize even when you weren't wrong sets the atmosphere for healing and restoration in a relationship that you value. Who was wrong isn't the biggest concern, yet who is willing to invest in their own surrounding does.

One of the main reasons I speak of others in reclaiming your worth is because we live in a world where other people in some shape, form or fashion will have to interact with us. Whether they will work for us or we will work for them.

There is an old term that says that we ought to treat others the way we want to be treated. That means that those we encircle ourselves with is a direct reflection of who we are and how we value ourselves. Demonstrating self-discipline is a strength that many of us do not have.

Self-discipline reflects maturity, class, distinction and over all control. I admire athletes, especially those women that are in the fitness competitions. These women practice a strict diet and exercise regiments. They get to bed early and start their fitness plan very early in the morning with food preparation and exercise. This kind of discipline is extremely hard; however, they live for the results of their practice. How much more can we achieve from a personal, spiritual and professional stand-point if we become more disciplined?

We need to be driven by results. Results help in deciding if we are using the best practices for our lives. People that are self-disciplined in all areas of their lives reduce risk; have larger bank accounts, a healthier mind/body and soul. Self-disciplined people are focused on the results at hand and in the end they have a clearer outlook on the direction of their life and who should fit in it.

Another very important characteristic to increase your self-worth is embodying integrity. Integrity is a big one for me. Integrity says you will do the right thing even if no one is watching. Having integrity in the times we live in now is a star quality. Being able to sleep at night because you have done your absolute best and treated others fair and honest is a joy to admonish.

Being whole and undivided, that is powerful in itself. To be whole means nothing is broken. This is a quality that very few can admit that they honestly possess.

We are quick to judge a pastor or person of the holy cloth when they make mistakes but when it comes to our lives, we cannot say that we have done our best at exemplifying integrity. This is one sure way to increase not only your self worth but also your value to others.

Honoring your core values is one of the main components of setting standards or a road map for your life. Values are often set for you beginning in your early years and transferred down from your parents or guardian.

This would be the perfect world and these times are seen less and less in today's society. So as we find our own way, it is crucial to set parameters and non-negotiables for our lives.

For instance, not dating married men under any circumstance or not drinking and driving. Other for sure ways to reclaim your self-worth is being bold enough to not let others misuse or mistreat you.

Know your value and know that there is only one of you, which makes you a valuable commodity.

Maintaining a positive attitude to the best of your ability is also key. One way to maintain a positive out look on life is to govern what is entered through your ears and eyes. Theses gates shape our perspective thus creating our reality. Surround yourself with only positive people, music and positive environments.

Enhance your energy by practicing sowing seeds into others that will increase their lives is also a way to add to your own reserve bank.

Take your destiny into your own hands by defining what success is for you.

Make SMART goals a smart goal is Specific, Measurable, Achievable, Realistic, and Time-bound that will keep you focused. Consider quality verses quantity.

Lastly choose you. Choose to be happy even in the face of adversity and let your vision be the fuel of your passion. Decisions don't need to be made on the fly. Take time to evaluate your options. Get a trusted advisor and run the idea past her or him and in the end, make better life decisions that add significance to your life.

## *Frame Your World With Your Words*

**REPEAT:**

*All is not lost.*

*I am worth more than what my past dictates.*

*I choose me.*

*My Smart Goals?*

*Specific. Measurable. Attainable.*

*Realistic. Timely.*

# CHAPTER TEN:

*A Voice for the Voiceless*

**Overcoming to Legacy**

Over the years, I endured and I did it silently. This silent behavior left me completely alone and misunderstood for a long time. Even when my faith found me, I was silent because I felt I couldn't show how broken I was to others. I experienced a lot of hurt during those years. I always felt like I didn't fit in most crowds, but I learned that I was created to stand out, and now I do it effortlessly.

I knew for over 17 years that this would be my work, but I had no intentions of revealing my own truths. I just wanted to be an advocate for those that suffered in silence. However, I quickly began to understand that this work was about more than just me.

This work was about connecting with other women and speaking up for the little girl who suffered within me. I didn't realize how important the little girl within me was until I had my second son. I wanted a girl so bad that I became depressed when I found out it was a boy.

I wanted a girl because I thought this was the only way to get it right, because I failed the little girl in me. I found that I didn't need to let her die. I could still preserve her and make her proud. I could be a voice for her when no one else was. For that little girl, I broke my silence.

It was scary at first, intimidating, challenging and of course, it brought up old feelings. Yet this is what I needed to do for her and for the many thousands of little girls that didn't believe that they could break their silence.

Being a voice for the voiceless has been encouraging for many who may not even have the same story but those who have lived behind a mask and dealt with the pain of hurt and secrets. I am grateful that not only did I overcome, but I won't be forgotten when I leave this earth because I am now writing my legacy.

My Pastor, Ervin Henderson, used to say "it's not the two dates on your tombstone that matter but the dash in the middle." When I truly found my dash, my purpose in life, my legacy, and my passion, I started to genuinely live. When you know why your life was pardoned, you begin to do what you are called to do regardless of money. Finding your voice in life can be a journey that can take several decades for many of us.

From abuse to abundance. We never know the path that has been set out for us until we get to the end of the road where the next road meets. We all have a story and for many reasons we hold it inside and deal with the pain of it all alone. When we open our mouths and remove the shame, we begin conversation and dance with a new reality.

This new reality is one that reflects the scars of our souls, yet the beauty of healing. I found a courage that I have never experienced before when I decided to share my truths. There is strength in surviving. Many did not.

What will your legacy be? How will you cultivate the youth by sharing your wealth of knowledge? Through my journey I had to decide what I would share and how much of it. I now understand that it's easy for the world to forgive a person that has been a victim of child abuse, domestic violence or sexual abuse.

However, there is another level of strength that it takes to disclose your secrets. Being a woman of the night or the woman that sleeps with married men is so degrading. Yet, this is my story, and I am so proud and thankful to God that I was freed from that web of bondage. The shame alone was enough for me to keep inside and in secret.

That is not the legacy I want to leave behind. I want to leave a legacy that convicts the hearts of those that I come in contact with to want to do more with their lives. There are some simple steps to go from overcoming to legacy status. Many were shared in this book.

First, understand what legacy is. Leaving Evidence of Greatness and Abundance while Cultivating the Young. There was a time where I taught dance to 43 students at my church and although the kids grew up and distance and years separated us, I knew the kids were still watching Ms. Rhonda. I have kept in contact with my dancers as they served a valuable purpose in my life on my road to self-discovery.

The kids, now adults, watched my behavior on social media. I was always conscious of their presence and how I portrayed myself. If for no one else, there were young people still looking to me for direction now as a young adult, and they want to ensure that what they had with me was genuine and authentic. We must cultivate the youth!

This is where the rewards of your labor are seen and where you know that you have made a difference in someone's life. If a child can grow up with you in mind when they think of a role model, give glory to God for purpose.

Decide today to forgive and prepare your store house for the new, the good, and the purpose. Without clearing the baggage in your closet, you will fail to live an abundant life.

Abundance in every area of your life is true living. Remove your mask if not for someone else do it for yourself. What are you good at? What turns you over at night? What would you do even if you didn't get paid for it? That my dear, is your purpose, calling for your attention. You're like a tree with many branches, and a healthy tree bares much fruit. Just like the tree, you are strong and although you may waver, you will not be broken. If you are planted in a rich soil with the right amount of love, forgiveness, water and sun, you will produce fruit after your own kind. When leaving a legacy or a mark on this earth, consider the many lives that you will impact. With your story, your message, your product, your book or simply your life, you can make a difference.

This life is bigger and there is so much more in store for you! Share yourself with those that are waiting on a seed from you so they too can flourish.

Life is about sowing and reaping. Some call it karma, but this is the true cycle of life. Make a decision to be free from the pain that binds you and leave evidence of greatness while cultivating the youth.

**Psalms 1:3 NLT**

*They are like trees planted along the riverbank, bearing fruit each season. Their leaves never wither, and they prosper in all they do.*

**Jeremiah 17:8 NLT**

*They are like trees planted along a riverbank, with roots that reach deep into the water. Such trees are not bothered by the heat or worried by long months of drought. Their leaves stay green, and they never stop producing fruit.*

# CONCLUSION

Many times we go through life without the proper tools to succeed, but if we slow down and dig deep, we will commit to greatness within ourselves. That one thing within each of us is given from God. That one thing is all that is needed to forgive, to hope, and to succeed. It's love.

God is love and with him, all things are possible to them that believe. With God we get clarity, and clarity makes decision making much easier. Choose love today. Love yourself, and the love for God will help you to love your enemies, even when they don't deserve it.

Be silent no more. What you endured has made you stronger. You have the power to speak the reality you want to see. Only speak the words for the world that you want to live in. Old ways of doing things will not open new possibilities.

Handle those old hurts and pains, so that you can be complete and whole, wanting nothing. Everyone wants to be seen for the work they do, but being a public success and a private failure make a recipe for loneliness. Not only should you speak life but also sow seeds that produce life and not death.

**Proverbs 18:21 KJV**

*Death and life are in the power of the tongue: and they that love it shall eat the fruit thereof.*

This was my grandparent's home. It is filled with memories and most importantly with love. Because of the love that was shed for me, I am reminded that I am a survivor.

**Dear Survivor,**

*Today I think of you.*

*I just want to tell you how excited I am to know you.*

*You are amazing and fabulous because you have not allowed those scars to define your beauty.*

*I am so proud of you for having the courage to use your voice and to not allow someone else's dysfunction to silence you.*

*You should be proud that you have chosen yourself over someone else's desire to kill you.*

*Because you're strong you wouldn't let them win.*

*You fought well and the prize goes to you.*

*Remember, it's not your fault.*

*And so today you live.*

*Congratulations, you are a survivor.*

                                          Rhonda A. Thompson

*And he shall be like a tree planted by the rivers of water, that bringeth forth his fruit in his season; his leaf shall not wither; and whatsoever he doeth shall prosper.*

**Psalms 1:3**

# R.O.S.

After changing my life, I had a desire to do something more to positively impact my world.

I became a volunteer for a domestic violence shelter called the Sojourner Truth House. It was there, that I personally began to help families by helping them to escape abusers by purchasing Greyhound tickets to another city.

One particular night, I felt a heavy sense of burden and I was moved to do more. I took ownership of this urge. After 15 years of running, I incorporated Rose of Sharon.

Rose of Sharon is a domestic violence organization that currently provides supportive services to women and children of domestic violence. Our goal is to be able to provide emergency shelter, transitional living and ultimately permanent housing. We are very excited about being a source to our community in the Greater Metro Atlanta, Georgia area and abroad. Please consider partnering with us to change the lives of many.

# ACKNOWLEDGEMENTS

My beloved late grandfather Shalie Wright was an amazing man, grandmother Christine Wright, Late Uncle Kenny Wright, my two remarkable boys Quincy Ricardo Wright and Dylan Thompson, you're the reason I am a voice for the voiceless.

My family Renee and Maurice Drane, Leo and Liz Wright, Cameron, Shonda, Cassandra, and Annette Wright, Beverly and Robert Allen and my best friend and sister Cleopatra White, thank you for always cheering me on, believing in me and supporting me.

There are many amazing women that have encouraged me to be the best version of myself.

The late Toi Taylor, Dana World Patterson, Pastor Melva Henderson, Darlene Thompson, Heidi B. Fuller, Pastor Pamela Hines, Jerhonda McCray,

Tahani Williams, Quinn Whatley, Lei-sa Anderson, Sharon Medina and Felicia Washington.

My only mother in this entire world whom I love dearly, Regina C. Cruz, I thank you all for being amazing examples to model my life after and because of you, I am who I am.

# ABOUT THE AUTHOR

Rhonda A. Thompson, "A Voice for the Voiceless" is an astonishing empowerment speaker, advocate, and author, who informs, motivates and empowers women of all walks of life to live purposefully. She is also a champion for victims and struggling survivors of domestic violence and abuse. Rhonda is dedicated to helping others to see their options and their potential to ultimately find their freedom.

A Milwaukee, Wisconsin native, born July 23, 1975, Rhonda transitioned from survivor to overcomer with focus and determination. She earned her Bachelor's Degree in Business Management and became the CEO & Founder of Rose of Sharon Transitional Living for Women, Inc.

As an ordained minister, Rhonda uses her voice, her experience, and her education to enlighten others and release them from the pain of domestic violence. Epitomizing the "my sister's keeper" charge, Rhonda is dedicated to helping all women to transform, renew, recover, and restore every aspect of their lives, and she takes pleasure in empowering others to know their God-given birth right and walk in their divine destiny.

Not only does Rhonda speak to any subject matter from her personal experiences, but she also brings an incredible level of professionalism and expertise! Rhonda does much more than talk and quote statistics; her events bring laughter through tears and focus on healing and restoration. Through a myriad of personal stories of survival of domestic violence; becoming an entrepreneur; running multiple businesses; marriage, motherhood, and more those engaged will be inspired, enlightened, uplifted and encouraged.

Mrs. Thompson had the privilege of beginning her domestic violence work in 1988 while manning the crisis hotline at "Sojourner Truth House" in Wisconsin. She also worked with "Brothers Against Domestic Violence" as a female body guard who escorted women to court for domestic violence cases.

As a survivor of multiple forms of abuse, including sexual abuse, she can understand a victim's perspective. Rhonda became an intricate part of the healing process for many women and uses her survivor platform to help others.

Her life's mission is to eradicate the senseless physical, emotional, and mental damage, injuries, and deaths that occur as a result of abuse and domestic violence.

Even though recent domestic violence incidents among globally recognized celebrities has become newsworthy coverage and spiked social media outrage, Rhonda is making it clear that domestic violence and abuse are not a new trend. Her comprehensive knowledge of domestic violence and its affects on the victims, businesses, the health industry, and the criminal justice system continues to be an essential resource for prevention and intervention.

Rhonda's passion for event planning has been an extraordinary masterpiece and an opportunity for her to foster domestic violence awareness while enlightening and entertaining her guests.

She is the creator and accomplished facilitator of several successful events, such as the Living Behind the Mask Masquerade Gala, which honors survivors of domestic violence and Tea Party Socials, which bring women together to engage in deep conversations with hopes of creating social change and healing.

All of these events are fundraisers designed to not only benefit ROS but also to raise consciousness, bring the community together in support of other survivors, and leave her guests with a sense of awareness and an experience that will last a lifetime.

To book Rhonda Thompson for your company training, special event or church or women's conference:

Email: RhondaAThompson@RosATL.org
Website: www.RhondaAThompson.com
Rose of Sharon: www.RosATL.org

TO CONNECT WITH RHONDA VIA ALL
SOCIAL MEDIA PLATFORMS:

Facebook, Instagram, Twitter and LinkedIn:
RhondaAThompson
Periscope: RhondaAThompson75

**Photo Credit:** Prime Phocus

# ENDNOTES

Cherie Burbach. "10 Myths About Forgiveness". About, Inc. December 23, 2015. http://friendship.about.com/od/Forgiveness/tp/10-Myths-About-Forgiveness.htm

Urban Dictionary. "Spill the Tea." 1999-2016. http://www.urbandictionary.com/define.php?term=spill%20the%20tea

National Center on Domestic & Sexual Abuse. "Domestic Violence Personalized Safety Plan." Accessed June 5, 2016. http://www.ncdsv.org/images/DV_Safety_Plan.pdf

Attorneys for Survivors of Childhood Sexual Abuse. "WARNING SIGNS OF CHILD MOLESTATION." Accessed May 5, 2016. http://www.childmolestationvictims.com/for-parents/

Crimes Against Children Research Center. "CHILDHOOD SEXUAL ABUSE FACT SHEET." May, 2005. http://www.unh.edu/ccrc/sexual-abuse/

Jewish Coalition of Domestic Abuse. "Cycle of Abuse." Accessed June 5, 2016. http://www.awarenow.org/www/docs/127

Safe Horizon. "National Domestic Violence Stats". Accessed on May 15, 2016.

http://www.safehorizon.org/page/domestic-violence-statistics--facts-52.html

All State Foundation. "Domestic Violence." Accessed on May 25, 2016.

https://www.allstatefoundation.org/domestic_violence.html

Holy Bible: New International Version. Grand Rapids, MI: Zondervan, 2005. Print.

IF YOU OR SOMEONE THAT YOU KNOW IS DEALING WITH DOMESTIC VIOLENCE, PLEASE VISIT THE NATIONAL DOMESTIC VIOLENCE WEBSITE AT

WWW.THEHOTLINE.ORG

OR CALL

1-800-799-7233.

www.ingramcontent.com/pod-product-compliance
Lightning Source LLC
Chambersburg PA
CBHW070621300426
44113CB00010B/1607